1015002071

291.42 BIE
Biermann, Derek.
Samadhi : personal journeys
to spiritual truth / Derek
KAMLOOPS LIBRARY

D0933722

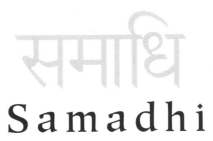

Samadhi

Samadhi

Personal Journeys to Spiritual Truth

DEREK BIERMANN

SHAMBHALA
BOSTON
2000

Thompson-Nicola Regional District
Library System
300 - 465 VICTORIA STREET
KAMLOOPS, B.C. V2C 2A9

For my loving wife Karyna

Shambhala Publications, Inc.
Horticultural Hall
300 Massachusetts Avenue
Boston, Massachusetts 02115
www.shambhala.com

© 2000 by Derek Biermann

All rights reserved. No part of this book may be
reproduced in any form or by any means, electronic
or mechanical, including photocopying, recording,
or by any information storage and retrieval system,
without permission in writing from the publisher.

9 8 7 6 5 4 3 2 1

First Edition

Cover design: Caroline de Fries
Design: Caroline de Fries and Kirsten Smith
Colour separations: Chroma Graphics, Singapore
Printed in Singapore by Tien Wah Press

∞ This edition is printed on acid-free paper that meets the
American National Standards Institute Z39.48 Standard.

Distributed in the United States by Random House, Inc.,
and in Canada by Random House of Canada Ltd

Library of Congress Cataloging-in-Publication Data

Biermann, Derek.
    Samadhi : personal journeys to spiritual truth / Derek Biermann.
        p. cm.
    ISBN 1–57062–579–4 (cloth)
    1. India—Religion. 2. Samadhi. 3. Spiritual life. 4. Saints—
    India—Portraits. I. Title.

BL2003 .B54 2000
291.4'2—dc21

99–088975

1015002071

Contents

Preface

If we agree that the aim of practice on a spiritual path is to reach the destination of perfect inner peace, to achieve a depth of understanding beyond our limitations, to place ourselves into a more expansive context within our own consciousness, and to find answers to the eternal questions of self-inquiry, then India has much to offer us if we are humble enough to receive.

The path of faith in India is a path well worn by the enlightened, the illuminated, the self-realized, the detached, the austere, the renounced, and the fully surrendered for over four thousand years. The Holy Vedas are the oldest known scriptures in Indian literature and were composed in Sanskrit many hundreds of years before the birth of Christ. The concluding portion of the Vedas are made up of spiritual treatises of varying length called the Upanishads. They form the philosophical basis of Vedanta and are widely regarded as the principal authority of Hinduism. The Bhagavad-Gita, "The Song of God," constitutes the sixth book of the great Indian cultural epic, the Mahabharata, and contains in its text the very essence of Vedic knowledge. During that same period Siddhartha Gautama, later known as the Buddha, achieved enlightenment under the Bodhi tree in Bodh Gaya and announced his realization of Nirvana. No matter whether one has a belief in God, the true Self, or formless consciousness; nor whether one is advanced in spiritual awareness or at the beginning of inquiry; nor to which religious order or doctrine one feels an attachment — India accommodates all who embrace her.

At the deepest and most advanced level of meditation there is an effortless, limitless, and ego-less state of transcendence that is described as a direct experience of the conscious Self. This is *samadhi*. *Samadhi* is considered to be the ultimate spiritual reality. Scientific theory and logic make no sense of this phenomenon. It is a state in which every cell in the body is said to remain unchanged, as if suspended in time. In *samadhi* the devotee experiences altered physiological conditions that include the cessation of breath, pulse, and sleep over periods of hours or days. *Samadhi* is beyond the mind, beyond thinking and understanding. To enter into the experience of *samadhi* is to enter into higher realms of consciousness. At the highest level of *samadhi*, the manifest and transcendent reality merge to become indivisible from the Self. *Samadhi* is a word that, when spoken in the company of seers, mystics, and ascetics alike, commands deep reverence and respect.

A spiritual life is a creative process, a path of devotion, and a journey of self-discovery. Within these pages we are presented with a rare and privileged insight into the sacred lives of sincerely devoted people in northern India as they answer questions about their beliefs, their spiritual practices, and *samadhi*. The subjects of these portraits were all asked the same specific questions outlining their spiritual experiences. Each individual was asked:

What is faith?
What is truth?
What is reality?
What is love?
What is *samadhi?*

With their blessing, the answers to these and other questions were recorded, transcribed, and are presented here as a series of comparative monologues. The text varies little from the original conversations, with only minor changes to grammar for the sake of clarity and fluidity. Sanskrit and Arabic words that appear in the text have been italicized, with the exception of names of people, places and spiritual groups, and words that are widely used in English.

As a medium with which to express creativity, photography communicates ideas and ideals through a process of observation in a visual language. To communicate in this language has given shape to my experience of life and led me on a transcendental journey of self-discovery. What manifested through a personal transformation has ultimately resulted in the blissful emergence of my spiritual consciousness.

Accepting the world as the camera records it is not the same as having an understanding of it. For that experience we have to go deeper in our perception. Looking beyond their physical characteristics, the subjects of these portraits were selected for their innate spiritual qualities and practices. A relationship based on mutual trust and understanding was established prior to any photography taking place, usually after several meetings. The subjects were all photographed in natural light, and within the context of their immediate surroundings.

What intrinsically binds the subjects into this collection of portraits is their faith. This book seeks to illuminate such qualities, emerging from the hearts and minds of these sincerely devoted people. Through the portraits and accompanying text, we look at the sacred practices of Hindus, Tibetan Buddhists, Christians, and Muslims. Some of the devotional practices, including self-chastisement and self-mortification, may appear extreme and severe, until we understand that these acts are performed as selfless acts of faith. The emphasis is not on the infliction of pain, but rather on the belief that faith is stronger than pain. The knowledge and wisdom of these people serve to guide us to a clearer understanding of the depth of devotion in India.

There are many spiritual paths leading to the same destination in India. *Samadhi*, Nirvana, and Heaven are representative of the highest Reality; they embrace the ultimate consciousness and the supreme liberation of enlightenment. We are all at different stages on the path; only consciousness separates us from deeper awareness and insight. Once an understanding of the relationship between the self and the universe has been realized, Reality becomes crystal clear as our timeless nature is revealed.

True spirituality is not in full view in India. It remains obscured to the insensitive and the disrespectful; it requires a genuine desire and the purest intention from the seeker. Along our path in search of the truth, we are reminded that what is revealed to us is always in accordance with our own level of understanding and devotion.

I greet the divine that dwells within you.

DEREK BIERMANN

Annapurna Devi

B. BIHAR

The only known living female saint in the holy city of Vrindavan, Annapurna Devi has been chanting her mantra for up to sixteen hours every day for the past twenty-five years. Annapurna's guru and her grandfather's guru were the same man, a direct descendant of the fifteenth-century saint, Caitanya Mahaprabhu. She is known to go into a weeping trance during meditation that can last for several days.

"The only way to Krishna is to surrender yourself; that is all, nothing else. Faith comes from your heart. If you are offering only a little flower to him, he accepts with fullest love if there is real love with your offering. One calls for Krishna sincerely. I call for Krishna weepingly. Weep for Krishna and he appears.

Truth is he who speaks the truth. One who believes in truth will only speak the truth; and with truth in your heart, love will come immediately. Where there is no truth, there is no love. Truth is necessary where Krishna lives; and where he lives, happiness lives. He is perfect. When I chant, by the grace of my guru, Krishna enters into my heart and gives me much pleasure. I forget to eat and drink and I even forget to sleep — I forget everything. Good devotees are now very rare on this earth."

Rajeshwarananda Giri

B. Ayodhya

On the sandy banks of the River Ganges in Rishikesh, there stands a large rock. Into the side of this rock a small shelter has been constructed. Rajeshwarananda Giri, who built the dwelling, has been living there for the past eight years. The only time he leaves is during the monsoon season, when the river rises and floods his home. He said the rock is where he spends most of his life in devotion and meditation.

"From time immemorial we are related to God and devoted to God. Even in my childhood, I left home as a boy with one-pointed determination: to find and see God. Thinking and meditating and reflecting on the soul is my spirituality. Our relationship to God is that of individual spirit souls and we are forever united with *paramatman*, the supreme Self. We are eternally related to God, and devotion can lead to the realization of God.

This rock is named Anandeshwar Maha Dev, and on the roof there is a *linga*,[1] which is the blissful Shiva. This is where I perform my spiritual practices based on karma, devotion, and knowledge. To meditate on the imminent and whole encompassing reality, that is my yoga. I am the same as God, omnipresent in my consciousness. I am Brahman, which is pure and eternal consciousness. Brahman is truth, but if we inquire deeply, this existence is illusion. Only the spirit is true; the body is illusion. Spiritual consciousness is only one and can never be divided. To have one-pointed concentration and devotion toward that one reality, that itself is the highest principle. My guru is the *dandi*,[2] Swami Hansananda, who lives up there on the hill. He has given me knowledge and I am developing that knowledge."[3]

---

1 Carved phallic symbol.
2 A master who has earned the privilege of carrying a stick.
3 Hindi–English conversation interpreted by Ashwin Rao.

Kamal

B. Madras

Kamal was raised in Mumbai and received a typically western education. After completing his third year at university studying English literature and ancient Indian cultural history, Kamal was forced to leave home due to a sudden change of circumstances. He traveled throughout India on a spiritual search that finally led him to Rishikesh. A passing saint from Mathura made such an impression on Kamal, that he immediately took the vows of spiritual initiation.

"I am a *sadhaka*, which literally means one who is doing *sadhana*, which are spiritual practices. I am a *baba*, a devotee, but here I am called a beggar. In our spiritual tradition, *babas* are not supposed to work. We can do selfless service in a temple or an ashram, but we cannot do any work or business because making business always involves some form of lying and cheating. So I did selfless work in a temple here in Rishikesh for fifteen years, sweeping and cleaning in exchange for a bed and meals. Every day, I practiced yoga and chanted my mantra. I did my *sadhanas* in the name of God. Now they can no longer offer me a place to stay, so I am out on the street, reduced to begging in order to eke out a most basic existence. I sleep under the stars at night and live a simple life of contemplation.

When I was twenty-five, a living saint arrived here from Mathura and gave a most impressive public lecture and demonstration of his *siddhi*.[1] His experience of the Self was as unbroken consciousness and, by a mere glance or touch, he could help the spiritual aspect of anyone he was in contact with. A living saint is a person who has realized the Self and is able to live in the Self each and every moment. Those were the rare ones, of a caliber that is not seen anymore — the whole tradition is finished with now. What he showed us I had never experienced in my life, because he performed it through telepathy — inside my head and to all the others there. I was immediately initiated into spiritual life and it was a wonderful experience. It is something that has never been repeated in my life, not even compared with later experiences like seeing 'the light'; 'the blazing light of a thousand suns.' I know now that they were not important experiences, although it was common for anyone doing *japa* yoga, which was my practice. *Japa* yoga is the chanting of the Divine Name and one has to be initiated into it, which I was by my guru. A mantra is personally handed down from the guru to the disciple, and that mantra is never revealed or the power is gone. It is called the *bija* mantra, the seed mantra that leads one to the presiding deity like Krishna, Ganesh, or Hanuman.

Basically, there are three levels of *japa* yoga. For sixteen years I was at the first level, which was verbal chanting. Sometimes I would chant continuously all day and occasionally for days together. I used to chant my mantra with my *mala*[2] and I would count: one hundred and eight mantras made a complete *mala*. Ten *malas* made one *purita charana*, which totaled one thousand and eighty. Then you counted one hundred and eight *purita charanas* to make one *kumbha*. If you chanted one hundred and eight *kumbhas* of your mantra, then God should appear before you in the form of the presiding deity. After sixteen years of audible chanting, I began the second level of *japa* yoga, which is semi-audible. My tongue would move, but words would not form because it was becoming a more and more

internal experience. By the third level, no words were uttered. The *japa* had become clear sound and then the mantra stops. It is a perfect state of calmness and peace in which you understand that our true nature is pure and eternal consciousness. When I reached that sound of silence, the *japa* fell away because I no longer needed it; the mantra was omnipresent.

One day I stopped chanting. I had uttered my mantra millions, probably billions, of times, but no deity appeared before me. I gave up *japa* yoga and took the path of self-inquiry instead, after reading the complete works of Swami Vivekananda, Ramakrishna Paramahamsa, Sri Ramana Maharshi, and Sri Aurobindo. Their words so impressed me, showing me a way out of the suffering I was in. I realized that there is an imminent Reality which is pure and eternal, which has nothing to do with time and space. I rejected all the deities and demi-gods like Rama and Vishnu and Shiva. Deities do not satisfy me at all; for me they are not truth, and they no longer exist for me.

What exists for me is beyond all that. What is clear to me now is the very nature of consciousness. I know that I am part of that reality, that I am not this body and not this mind — I have nothing to do with it at all. People speak of pure consciousness in the external, but the real meditation is internal — going to the source of the mind and remaining at the source of the mind. Individually, we identify with our individual minds, but we are only a part of the cosmic mind, which contains countless billions of thoughts. What exists for me is pure, eternal consciousness. There is this earth, the stars, and the moon — it is one creation. I feel that this creation is not really a creation, but an appearance of this consciousness. This world is only an appearance on the screen of pure consciousness, as was the appearance of so many other civilizations that came and went before ours. It is just like the appearance of a film we see on the cinema screen. We can see all kinds of things like love and death, war and happiness, but when the film is over, the screen returns back to like it was; that, I feel, is our true reality. Reality is that screen, and we are this eminent reality. Rebirth is explained as transmigration — many lives born many times before. We get indications and impressions of experiences from our previous lives — they are called *samskaras*. These *samskaras* are the latent tendencies from past lives which remain in our subconscious minds. One who has reached a state of pure consciousness is closest to God, because God is that very state of pure consciousness. Self-realization is the experience of the Self as unbroken consciousness."

1 Supernatural mystical abilities.
2 String of prayer beads.

Dr. Ondh Biharilal Kapoor

B. UTTAR PRADESH

The author of more than thirty books on spirituality in Hindi and English, Dr. Ondh Biharilal Kapoor is the former head of the Department of Philosophy at Agra University. A renowned scholar, he has retired to a quiet cottage in Vrindavan to continue his writing.

"Faith is something natural and it is contagious, especially when in the association of saints. My own spiritual life began almost from my birth — that was my *samskara*.[1] My parents were very spiritual and the environment in which I lived was conducive to faith, so it was a natural process for me from the start. I wanted other people to share my experiences, so I started writing. People have found faith after reading my books about the lives of saints. An example of this is a book I wrote entitled *The Saints of Bengal*. It has turned atheists into believers. Many people have written to me or come to meet me, to offer their gratitude for my helping them to find the path of faith. For some people faith is blind belief, but whether it is blind or not depends on the sincerity of the person. There are so many spiritual practices of so many kinds, but sincerity is the main thing. If you are sincere with yourself and if you are a sincere seeker of the truth, then your faith will be of the right type. You will not deceive yourself.

I feel that the purpose of life is to realize God. If a person dies without doing that, then the purpose of their life has been unfulfilled and wasted. My happiness with Krishna or God is totally indescribable and above everything else I could ever have experienced. Even those who are self-realized cannot describe their feelings, because they are on a different level. The saints are the ones truly and sincerely engaged in fulfilling the purpose of their lives, by realizing God irrespective of their caste or creed or nationality. Westerners are unfortunately lost in *maya*,[2] which is the opposite of truth. They have to turn their backs and face the light. It will be a new experience that will really open their eyes. There are people who believe in self-realization and others who believe in *jnana*,[3] but the path of wisdom and the path of devotion are different. The Self is already realized once you realize yourself as a real devotee of God. You do not have to realize yourself separately; that comes as a by-product and is a complete experience in itself. The type of love you have in your heart depends on the object or the person to which you are attached. Love, for me, means an intense attachment to God and the love I have for God, and I want to share this with others."

1   Subliminal impressions from past lives.
2   Illusion.
3   Knowledge.

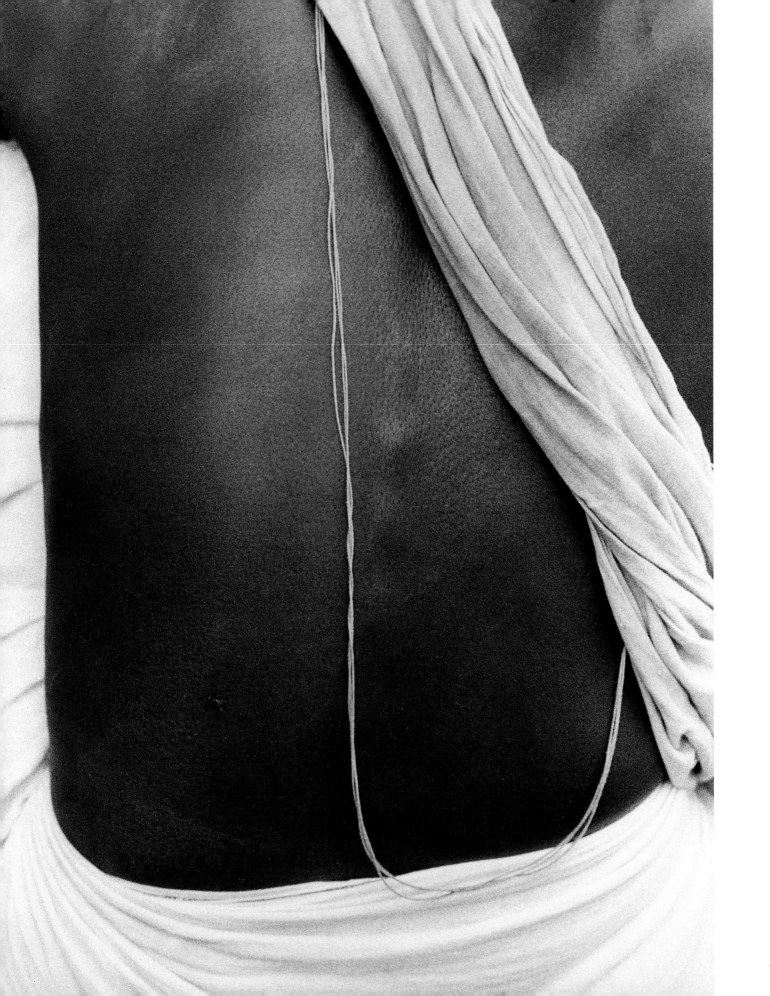

OM
This eternal word is all:
what was, what is and what shall be,
and what is beyond
in eternity.

MANDUKYA UPANISHAD

Ugen Dolma

B. LHOKHA, TIBET

Ugen Dolma is one of the more fortunate Tibetan Buddhist nuns — she managed to escape the Chinese occupation of Tibet, by crossing the Himalayan border into India on foot. Ugen, who speaks no Hindi or English, is being integrated into the Buddhist community at McLeod Ganj.

"Internal faith is something to do with your mind and your heart. I fully trust what His Holiness[1] says and I have complete faith in him. My feeling, according to my practices and knowledge of the 'four noble truths,'[2] is simple attachment and automatic faith. When I see pictures or *thanka*[3] paintings of Lord Buddha I automatically have feelings of happiness.

According to Buddhist teaching, there are the 'six realms of life' and they are forms of rebirth as we see it in the 'wheel of life.' The lowest rebirth is hell and there are many forms of hell; like the hell of fire and burning, and the hell of freezing in the coldness of ice. The next form of rebirth is to be reborn as an animal. This is followed by rebirth into evil spirits and titans, a human life, and finally the heavenly life.

The purpose of life is to get relief from these forms of rebirth and suffering, not only for yourself but for all human beings. I became a nun so as to be able to walk away from the human cycle of suffering in order to achieve the fullest enlightenment. I am so happy to be a nun, because I do not have to suffer like lay people, with so much anger and quarreling. I have no need to quarrel; I have happiness, and I pray for the happiness of all beings. Practicing Buddhism is both practical to this life and the next. I am always happy to be of help or service to anybody. For our good deeds in this life, we will bear the fruits in the next life.

In human life, just to be born is to suffer pain, until the final suffering which is death. This is explained in the teachings of Lord Buddha on suffering: to be born, illness, getting old, and finally death. It is so important for people to understand the law of karma. Our karma follows us into the next life and that life is even more important than this life, so we should follow the teachings of Lord Buddha and try to understand the meaning of happiness."[4]

1   His Holiness the Dalai Lama Tenzin Gyatso.
2   The basis of Buddhist teaching.
3   Tibetan painting on cloth.
4   This conversation was recorded in Tibetan with the kind assistance of Anila Dechen. It was later translated into English by Tsering Yang Kri at the Department of Religion and Culture, Central Tibetan Administration, Dharamsala.

Swami Anandadevanand Saraswati

B. BIHAR

A monk and teacher of meditation and yoga in Rishikesh for more than twenty-five years, Swami Anandadevanand Saraswati only teaches individual students. He lives alone in a small house surrounded by a garden and tall trees near the River Ganges. Swami Saraswati believes in a pure and simplified life.

"I do not believe in the commercialization of yoga or meditation. My students are sent to me by word of mouth and I teach them. I have my own light, and spiritual light is the Spirit entering into our souls. That is the blissful light itself, and that light is part of the universal light. Faith means a belief in something. In the past, many rsis[1] and saints and other enlightened people came and gave their own light and thoughts and created faith. When Christ preached his teachings and meditations, he was crucified. People took his life because he said he was the son of God. People said, 'You cannot be the son of God' and killed him. In India if you say, 'I am the son of God,' nobody would kill you. They would say, 'Yes, you are the son of God; we believe you are a part of God.'

In ancient times, the seers realized that our breath controls the mind. When the breath is not flowing correctly, the mind is disturbed. The seers developed a technique to control the *prana* and it is that *pranayama* that I teach. *Pranayama* means controlling the breath that gives us life force. When the breath is slow and silent, the mind becomes more balanced and quiet. We are all affected in different ways by our hormonal and glandular secretions. If you practice yoga the secretions become balanced; your entire body and personality becomes balanced too. That balance leads us closer to God. To say the word 'God' is to say: G(enerator), O(perator), D(estroyer).

There are many ways to *samadhi,* and for me the path is the *Astanga*[2] *yoga* I teach. Yoga has eight different aspects. These become clearer as progress is made into a higher consciousness through knowledge and practice of the *asanas*. When you sit in a particular posture, it is called an *asana* and it has many forms. The *astangas* begin with the five *yamas*, which teaches us about right behavior. They are non-violence, truthfulness, honesty, chastity, and non-attachment. This leads us to the five *niyamas*, which teaches us purity of life. They are contentment of the mind through meditation, practicing austerities, analyzing the self, purity of the mind, and surrender to God. Then the third *astanga* and the fourth, step by step, until you reach *samadhi*. The eighth and final achievement of yoga is *samadhi* — that is when your mind and your soul merge with the universal light.

Meditation means to take an internal journey. From when we are born we see only the external way. Meditation means to close your eyes and go inside to see your eternal light. Different meditation practices also balance the hormonal secretions. There are different techniques and they are all taught in a particular way, because there is a different approach for each individual, depending on their minds. From the ancient path and ancient teachings, and through my own experiences, we are taught how to select the mantra and the meditation for a particular person. The mantra is given only to you, which you keep in your mind for your contemplation. It is like a seed. If you put a seed in the ground, you do not have to open the ground to look; you have faith that it will grow automatically. Love is in your heart, where it has sensation and happiness. My life is perfect happiness."

---

1 Seers.
2 The name of the eight-limbed branch of yoga.

Tara Vasanti

B. PUNE

Born a Hindu Brahman, Tara Vasanti is a reiki master, painter, poet, and free-thinking "multi-dimensionalist." She describes herself as a "very basic, loving human female." Tara was in McLeod Ganj on a pilgrimage from Pune to attend the month-long public lectures of His Holiness the Dalai Lama Tenzin Gyatso.

"Spirituality, for me, means connecting with your greater Self. Everyone is their physical self nearly all the time, but when you start connecting to your greater Self, that is when you start realizing that you are a spiritual being, not just a physical being. Love is understanding the connection and then expressing it in hundreds of ways.

God is infinity, but viewed by our finite eyes. God is all that It is. Another name for God is: 'All that is.' We are multi-dimensional, simultaneous incarnations of our consciousness, except we don't see ourselves that way and that is where our disempowerment comes from. Ultimate philosophy talks about non-duality. The root of everything is only one. I will tell you where the first separation takes place: in the real and deep sense, there is only 'I.' 'I' knows that 'It' is: 'I am.' That's the first separation. 'It' knows that 'It' exists. The next separation is 'I' and 'you,' and so it goes on. So the root of 'It' is that there is only 'I.' That is called Absolute. Some people who think they have discovered enlightenment talk about knowing the Absolute.

The first phase of my life has been cleansing — taking care of issues that needed taking care of. My earth-oriented being was bringing forth the greater Self of myself and helping others to realize their greater Selves. So, in other words, in two halves — my earthly connections and my other-dimensional dimensions. Faith is knowingness, and knowingness can vary according to the person and according to the particular situation. You just know. There are no questions asked — there is nothing to analyze, no logic, and no reasoning needed — you just know. That is faith.

What I know now is the truth. I know that all truths are related truths. I understand that, so that tells me not to get stuck at any one truth. Anything is truth. Whatever the other person is saying is the truth. I take that into consideration when I am stating my truth. Having the conviction of what you know and what you understand. This way, my truth is becoming wider and wider. It's not one-pointed anymore; it has taken on length and depth and breadth. The same applies to multi-dimensionality. We have been used to thinking linearly, but now I understand that it's not in one line anymore but many lines, in different directions, and those directions each have many more directions. It has nothing to do with space. If you hold your fist tightly, that little space contains all the dimensions. Once I started thinking about this, many new doors opened.

Another thing that really opened my doors was the realization that I or we don't exist in reality; rather, that reality exists within us. When I first heard this, it really blew my mind! How was that possible? Then I started to realize that I am much, much more than who I thought I was. It's not just the physical me who I see in the mirror and who knows her name; that is only a tiny point of me and I have many more points of reference. I started to think and act from those other references. The more

I did, the more I realized that they were not only my other points of reference but were also me. That was because I understood that I am much more than who I thought I was. I began connecting with my greater Self and being it.

Multi-dimensionality is for me like a sphere and we are only one point of that sphere, but the other points are also you. The other points are not necessarily physical points; they could be different realities and higher dimensions. To explain what dimension is: it is the vibratory frequency at which you vibrate. Everything exists as vibrations, so the physical me has certain vibrations, but I also exist at other much higher vibrations. One thinks and acts differently from higher vibrations and your values change, your viewpoint changes, and the way you see other people changes. The benefit of realizing your multi-dimensionality is that your dealings with other people change; the interpretation of events and people around you changes. Once the interpretation changes, things get easier, simpler, and less complicated, and your viewpoint broadens.

I see myself as a blending of consciousnesses. When I started realizing and understanding things, I saw myself as one bead on a string of many and saw that all the beads on that string were my past, present, and future lives, and the string was the consciousness. Once I realized that, many things started to be revealed to me about the blending of consciousness. Sometimes it's such a blending that you see it as a number of consciousnesses, but it is only one — like a circle — and many roads meet at that circle. I have seven consciousnesses, seven roads that meet at the circle, and the circle is me. The advantage of this is that every road has access to the wisdom that I had or the experiences that I as Tara have had. In other words, it becomes a great exchange, one great extended family.

One of my seven consciousnesses is from a planet not from our universe; it's called Essassani. In our simple language, one of my future female aspects lives on Essassani. They are lighter beings than us and they are from our future. Essassanis don't have names. They don't have a language; they communicate telepathically. But we need a point of reference, a name to refer to ourselves, so I call my future self Reshma. Reshma means soft like silk, and at the same time strong. So Reshma is my Essassani self and I can relate to that name. I have learnt so much from the Essassanis. They are a very intellectual society. It's not only me; there are a few hundred people on earth right now who have Essassani connections. I just want to place them in the right context so that they are understood. There are many societies helping us earth human beings right now to go through our transformation; Essassanis are just one of them. They can tell us what to do, or how to do things differently, because they have lived on earth as human beings. That's the idea of blending consciousness. They made agreements with a number of earth consciousnesses to be human beings. In other words, we can then learn from each other, like exchange students. There are Essassanis on earth right now, but as human beings. Their consciousness is blended with human consciousness. They have learnt what it is to be human, so that is how they can come back and teach us.

It is not only Essassanis; we have connections with Pleidians and many other places to do with our transformation. As I know now, I have seven consciousnesses; three of them are earth-orientated and the other four are higher-dimensional. Perhaps what I am saying is too much, because not everyone would understand. People are used to being a certain way; they are used to that and they have been doing it very well. They are masters of being who they are right now, but it's time to expand and to consider other possibilities."

Nayab Mufti Abdul Hameed Naumani

Nayab Mufti[1] Abdul Hameed Naumani is the chief *imam*[2] of the Jama Masjid[3] in Agra. All Muslim holy men expressed their reluctance to be photographed. It was explained to me that because Allah has no face, to photograph the faces of His representatives may be misinterpreted. Mufti Naumani listened to my requests at length, before granting his rare permission to be photographed.

"Faith means to believe in Allah. Allah and God are the same. He gave us life, and what He wants I will do and what He wants for the future will also be done. I trust in Allah and nothing else. In the past, the present, and the future, Allah is always present. Allah is One and He has power, so what He wants will be done. The sky and the earth are in His hands; the whole universe is His. Allah sent us holy books, and what is written in the Holy Koran[4] is the truth. Truth must follow you everywhere, while you are sleeping or eating or working. You should have the name of Allah in your heart and put your trust in Him. Mohammed was the last prophet and he showed what is written in the Holy Koran, and every word that is there is one hundred percent correct. To be a good Muslim means to trust and follow the advice written in our holy book. Truthfulness and honesty are most important.

We have five 'pillars of faith' and they are instructions from Allah to teach humans the correct way in life. The first is *shahadah*, which means true belief and conviction in the knowledge that He is the only One. The second is *salah*, which is prayer, and that means to pray five times every day. The third is *zakah*, which is your transactions in business and giving to charity. If you have excess wealth, you have to share your wealth by helping poor people and beggars. At the end of every year, two-and-a-half percent of your money must be given away as a donation. You do not give that money to family members unless you have a sister or a brother who lives outside your home and who is poor; then you can pay them something. Otherwise, you must give outside your family first. The fourth is *sawm*, which is your way of living with your customs and strict fasting in the month of Ramadan. During Ramadan, you pray and fast. You should eat before sunrise, and for the whole day until sunset you should not take food or water. There should also be no sexual meeting with a woman. The fifth is *hajj*, which means to make a pilgrimage to Mecca at least once in your lifetime. This is the function of Islam and the five important points to remember.

Islam does not have any symbols except the star and the moon. People will only be misguided, because Allah is One and He is invisible. Why think about what shape He comes in? You feel His power and that is enough. Without a guide in this world, no-one can reach the home of Allah. He sent prophets into the world to tell people to believe in the Koran and to trust in Allah and help each other to know Allah. If we follow this way, then happiness will come to all humanity. If you follow His instructions, then everything will come to you.

One day the whole world will be finished. The moon and the sun will be finished. This will happen when the greater percentage of people who do not believe in Allah believe more in the material world. People will ask Allah to forgive them for any bad actions before they surrender their bodies. When we die, we will never be born again; there is no rebirth. In that last moment when you die, if you did good you will go to heaven and if you did bad then you will go to hell. The karma will be calculated and weighed. Hell is a place of cheating and insults and abuse and dishonesty, and heaven is a place of peace and happiness and love."[5]

1 A position of religious authority in Islam.
2 A leader of Islamic prayer.
3 Friday mosque or main mosque of a city.

4 The holy book of Islam.
5 Urdu–English conversation interpreted by Mohammed Kashif Khan.

Radhika Das Kathiya Baba

B. UTTAR PRADESH

Radhika Das Kathiya Baba was initiated and became a *sadhu*[1] at the age of eight. As a Kathiya Baba,[2] he has worn his *langoti*[3] for more than half his life. He was at the Kumbha Mela to support and serve his guru, Avadh Bihari Das Kathiya Baba.

"This cult is so old and in this cult, *tapasya*[4] is very strong and important. The *langoti* gives us self-dependence. There is no need for clothing and no other help needed with anything. There are many benefits from wearing it; good sitting is not possible, much eating is not possible, and much sleeping is not possible. In every moment I am reminded about my faith through suffering; that is my work and my path. The physical body is nothing. The Neem tree is the holy tree for my cult, but this *langoti* is from Sisam wood, a very strong tree in India. I have worn mine for one completed period, which made good *bandha*.[5] If I wanted to open this belt it would be at that time. It was possible, but I wanted more years with my *langoti*, so I am going now for my second period of twelve years. It is my internal mirror, because I have taken this special way only for the truth. Inside and outside my body, everything shows that I am for God only. I am completely devoted to truth; that is why I keep my *jata*,[6] that is why I keep this *langoti* and use *tilak*[7] and chant my mantra and do my *tapas* every day. My practices remind me of my way to the truth.

The guru is the mirror. If you want to see your life and your faith with a mirror, then with your guru this is possible. The guru helps us to internalize with eyes wide open and to control the power ourself. The guru helps us like a mirror, and then we don't need the mirror anymore. The guru has more than one side — maybe four or six — but you only ever see one side. If you want to accept a guru, you must become a disciple completely. If the guru says fall down, then you fall down. How do you know if a guru is good for you? Here the principle is that the right student is always for the right guru.

We love Shiva, and Shiva loves the *sadhus*. Shiva also has many strong rules and regulations to follow. The first rule in becoming a *sadhu* is to go away from your family and lose everything material. If you don't want to follow rules, then you have to be away from here because to be a good *sadhu* is to follow rules. Faith is very easy when you are faithful. I am a little part of the big machinery that is God and this universe. He is represented in everything. Everyone has some special work; that is why we are all here. Why was I born? Why am I a *sadhu* in India, and why did you have your birth in another country? There is no difference between us, because God wants you there and me here. That is our destiny. It is only our own limitation that does not allow us to see this clearly. Life is only possible for me this way as a Kathiya Baba; it is God's wish. It is not my need or your need; it is God's need. Faith is a mental condition: with good faith comes good condition.

What is truth and what is a lie? Where do we find a lie? I have been a *sadhu* for twenty years, but I have never found a lie anywhere. Everything is true; it is part of the bigger machinery. If God wants you to lie, He is trying to explain the truth.

Everything has two sides, and we never see both sides of anything at the same time. So, what is a lie? How can we be sure? What is right if everything has two parts? You have to go deeper to see the whole picture. Maybe the lie is the truth? I am a representative of goodness and I work for God, so why do I need this body? I completely forget about this body and remember my internal self instead; that is the meaning of *samadhi*. When you are attached to the material world, how is *samadhi* possible? You have to completely forget the material aspect of yourself."

1 A holy person, an ascetic.
2 A term of respect for a holy man or spiritual master.
3 A chastity belt.
4 Penance or severe exercises.
5 Self-discipline or self-control.
6 Length of matted natural hair.
7 Sacred paint or clay.

Kapil Adwait Mahatma Yog Versha

B. Sikkim

Kapil Adwait Mahatma Yog Versha was primarily at the Kumbha Mela to be of support and service to Maha Yogi Pilot Babaji in his camp. She was at his side during all the important ceremonies and spiritual rituals that took place during the festival. Yog Vershaji is recognized as a living saint.

"Faith is that which works through our eternal heart, and that faith gives satisfaction to this life. Reality is truth, and truth never goes away; truth is truth. Everything seen in this existing world is not truth. The body itself is not truth, but the energy within the body is everlasting truth. The purpose of life is to understand and experience truth, and this body is the medium for reaching that destination. We have this human body to reach perfection and nothing else.

Religion is realization. The real meaning of religion is the realization of the true Self. I worry so much about the world and the misunderstandings of this life that lead to frustration and tension everywhere. The world only needs a better understanding of the mystery called life and there would not be so much suffering.

Until and unless we understand truth, we will not reach perfection, which is to become oneness and to merge with the Supreme Consciousness. We are in this body and we experience the world, but when we are in the heart our consciousness merges with the Supreme Consciousness. That is the understanding of pure love. Your heart will never be broken when you understand the true blissfulness inside you. Loving in a spiritual way is a divine love that requires an understanding of yourself. Through the process of meditation you can enter into yourself and see the conscience of your consciousness; that is when you see the face of *samadhi*. It is the Supreme Energy that sustains our bodies. A light bulb may appear to be 'dead,' but when the light is turned on, it gives the bulb life. It is the same with the Supreme Energy that gives light to our bodies. When the light is out, the body is 'dead.' The light is right there; you only have to look within to understand your inner consciousness."

Satyendra Narayan Singh

B. BIHAR

Satyendra Narayan Singh has been on a spiritual path since his eleventh birthday, and for the past eighteen years has been a devotee of his guru, Shree Shree 1008 Kapalika Mahakal Bhairwand Saraswati. Wearing a black robe to his feet, Narayan Singhji delighted in showing me photographs of his guru performing Tantric rituals in numerous graveyards at night.

"One day, many years ago, someone gave me a book. In that book there was a picture of my guru and his address. I knew, just from looking at his face, that he was my master and immediately went to the village to find my guru. When he saw me, he recognized me and gave me *diksa*[1] right on the spot. *Diksa* is like a wire between the heart of the devotee and the guru. Tantra and the mantra are both given to the disciple by the guru, and Tantra is a demonstration of the mantra. Tantra is a path that leads to the devotion of God. The shortest way between the devotee and the Godhead is through the guru. It is a way to reach God, like an aeroplane.

Black is the color that is related to Tantra in the highest position. Only a few wear these black robes and travel across the provinces doing Tantric work; it is a stage of seniority. When all the devotees meet together at night, we do so because the night is black and that is our special color. I cannot like the day, because hither and thither there are crowds and much quarreling. At night we are in a spiritual mood; it is a peaceful time for devotion. We cannot see except with Tantra; it is like a light to see the path of devotion in the darkness. You can die if you are afraid of Tantra when you practice it — it has powers that can easily kill a person. The spiritual faith in Tantra comes when we demonstrate the mantra; we see the truth in a hurry.

My guru lives far in the mountains and we don't like to come to the cities. He is only here for the Kumbh;[2] otherwise, you never see him. I have remained in the service of my guru here at the Kumbh for the past few months and I am so happy. Love is a pure thing; love, for me, is to be in the company of saints. With pure love in my heart, I am beyond the human prestige of things."

1 Initiation of a seeker into spiritual life.
2 Abbreviation of Kumbha Mela.

Mind is the forerunner of all actions.

All deeds are led by mind, created by mind.

If one speaks or acts with a serene mind,

happiness follows,

as surely as one's shadow.

THE BUDDHA

India Bharti

B. TASMANIA, AUSTRALIA

India Bharti is a Shaiva[1] and a Naga Baba;[2] he is also the maker of extraordinary music. His amplified wooden bow-like instrument is self-made and produces a unique sound, which he combines with voice. India Bharti was at the Kumbha Mela to see his *sadhu* friends and to live with other Naga Babas, taking part in the procession of the *sadhus* on the auspicious bathing days.

"I don't know about spirituality. I became a worshiper of Shiva nearly twenty years ago. Just by being like I am, people are seeing a worshiper of Shiva — that's all. Shaivas are quite easily distinguishable in appearance; they usually wear wooden *rudraksa*[3] and are covered in ash. According to the worship of Shiva, it is futile without the application of ash. I realized the principle completely, but there was still the inhibiting factor of putting ash on my body. It's quite hard to wear it all the time.

I'm a member of the Sri Panch Das Nam Juna Akhara, the old *akhara*.[4] It was started by Sankaracarya, who was a sort of Hindu reformer in the eighth century. He was an impersonalist who believed that Shiva is formless. He believed in the incomprehensibility of Shiva and started the Juna Akhara. There are three major orders of *sadhus* in the *akhara*: the Giris, the Puris, and the Bharatis, with a combined membership of about fifty thousand. Fewer than two thousand of these are Puris and there are only about five hundred Bharatis, so there really aren't that many of us. Each of the three groups has a completely different personality that doesn't show in their appearance but you can pick it in their behavior.

The minute I arrived here, I just really liked India. That was in 1970. It was pretty different then; no-one wore shoes, hardly anyone wore western clothing, and there were only a few cars and no motorbikes. I came to India by an intellectual process, because I think that Indian philosophy is far more advanced than anything in the West. Indian ideas have made an inevitable transfer to the West, particularly since books started being translated from Sanskrit into English in the mid-seventies. Gradually all the books will be translated. You only have to read a few of them and you will never see the world in the same way as you did before.

I've been traveling constantly since 1970, and in all I've spent about six-and-a-half years in India. The longest I've stopped anywhere was for about a year. My music is automatic; if I like it, I extend on it. My instrument is totally original. I just put it together one day and it has supported me for the past eleven years, three times around the planet.

My guru gave me my name at a Kumbha Mela. One day, he just spontaneously named me 'India Bharti' and the name stuck. My guru's name was Pashuram Bharti, a completely ash-covered *sadhu*. I was living with a group of *sadhus* at the time of my initiation. When I went to the following Kumbha Mela he was there, but by the following one he was dead. One of Shiva's names is 'the destroyer of love.'

Sometimes I have a little affection toward humanity. I like the *babas* I've been sharing a tent with for the past few months; they're all really nice.

I have no truth and no purpose. I'm very happy as I am."

1   A devotee of Shiva.
2   A sect of naked *sannyasis*.
3   Distinctive wooden beads worn by devotees of Shiva.
4   Regiment.

Madras Baba Krishna Das

B. KERALA

Madras Baba Krishna Das is a retired *sadhu*. For more than fifty years he wandered on spiritual pilgrimages throughout India, leading a strict life of asceticism. In his small quarters in the ancient holy city of Radha Kund, Madras Babaji lives as an invalid and relies on neighbors and friends to help him with his few needs.

"Faith is the Almighty. I am a Gaudiya Vaisnava[1] and I follow the way of Caitanya Mahaprabhu's thinking. He came in the fifteenth century from Bengal and was the incarnation of Krishna. He did not come alone; he came with other people who helped him spread the message of love for God. Faith, for me, consists only of Mahaprabhu and Lord Krishna.

All my life I was a *sadhu* wandering here and there, wherever Krishna sent me. I roamed all throughout India, but in 1989 I broke my other hip and that was that — no more wandering. I have been living here in Radha Kund, where Krishna played with his friends as a boy. Now I only chant the *Gayatri*[2] mantra, which I received at my second and proper initiation.

Let that adorable, full light of God,

enlighten us, who meditate on Him.[3]

Since I have been here at Radha Kund, I awake at midnight to begin my chanting. I chant until around eight every morning, then I rest. I am a fickle-minded *sadhu* and I cannot only compose myself for chanting, so I engage my mind by reading the books I have, again and again. I want to live with my last breath here and to leave my body while chanting. Krishna has provided that very nicely, because I have been bed-ridden these past nearly ten years. I am an eternal servant of Krishna and I am happy beyond my expectations."

1 A devotee of Vishnu.
2 Sacred Vedic verse from the Rigveda.
3 Spontaneously recited verse from memory by Madras Babaji.

Chandra Kala Pandey

B. Sikkim

An English student in Delhi, Chandra Kala Pandey is preparing to become a *sadhvi*.[1] When her studies are completed, Chandra plans to devote her life to serving humanity as she walks the land. A devotee of Maha Yogi Pilot Babaji, she was a guest at his camp for the duration of the Kumbha Mela in Haridwar.

"Faith means to have positive vision. Having faith leads me toward calm and constructive vision. It's a learning process. To go beyond yourself, on a pathway to reach the truth. That path of truth teaches me to speak and think clearly in society, with actions that make me feel whole.

Spirituality is the path of divinity. It develops the consciousness and purifies the mind. It is the science of self-discovery. Spirituality in humanity teaches true love — to grow and explore and benefit others. I never want to misuse my life energy, because I know that I am only a guest on this planet.

The purpose of my life is to become a savior to the hungry and poor people of the world. God is universal energy. God is omnipresent, omnipotent, and omniscient. All my life I have believed that I belong to the universal family, and I want to help this family because I see all people in this world with equal eyes. One question is very important to me and I want to find the answer to it one day: 'Who am I?'"

1   A female *sadhu*.

Those wise ones who see that

the consciousness within themselves

is the same consciousness

within all conscious beings,

attain eternal peace.

KATHA UPANISHAD

Maha Yogi Pilot Babaji

B. BIHAR

Maha Yogi Pilot Babaji is from a wealthy family, which enabled him to fulfill his boyhood dream of becoming a fighter pilot. A near crash thirty years ago changed the course of his life. With the rank of Captain in the Indian Air Force, Pilot Babaji resigned his post to follow a spiritual path. Today his name is well known for his numerous public displays of faith, including at least twenty-five demonstrations of *samadhi*, either submerged underwater or buried underground. As a fully Self-realized yogi, Pilot Babaji has many thousands of devotees throughout India, with ashrams in New Dehli and Naini Tal.

"In the Indian language we have the word *visvasa*. Its English meaning has three dimensions: faith, trust, and belief. What has happened in modern times is delusion, because belief means the same to the Christians, the Islamics, or the Hindus of this world. The word 'belief' is used, but the word has been exploited. Religions do not just want your dedication; they want full surrender and for you not to use your mind or your intelligence. What happens is that our minds become exploited, making way for the ideological slavery which has existed for hundreds and thousands of years before us. If you discover that something is no good, then that belief can be changed. Faith runs deeper than belief; faith has devotion, and trust has determination. Trusting becomes the route to realization, faith becomes the route to dedication, and belief becomes the route to transition.

In the spinal column there is an energy which moves in currents called *ida* and *pingala*. *Ida* is cool energy that flows on the left side, and *pingala* is on the right side where warm energy flows. Through the center of the spinal cord there is a most useful and creative energy called *susumna*. It is like a chemical reaction in quantum physics, but physicists have not gone far in their understanding. It is not visible and cannot be explained in scientific or medical terms. Through the practice of yoga and Tantric teachings, the route of the breath can be changed so that both nostrils breathe the positive and negative energy as one. The *pranic* and *apranic* breath is pushed down the spine where it becomes 'awakened' energy, enlightened and realized energy. That is *kundalini*. When the *kundalini* is liberated, it flows up the chakras until it reaches the highest chakra, the Brahma chakra — that is where *samadhi* is realized. Unless it is woken from its sleep, the *kundalini* energy lies sleeping like a serpent with its tail in its mouth. *Kundalini* is a new word; the old word was *jagadamba*. *Jagat* means the universe and *amba* is mother; the 'Mother Energy' of the universe. We exist; the whole universe is inside us and our bodies contain everything. E-mail and the Internet are now here, but they have found out nothing new really. We are all 'internetted' within. Once you become at one with your Self, you are 'internetted' to the wide universe in a single second. We are the grouping and organization of physical senses, mental senses, celestial senses, and cosmic senses.

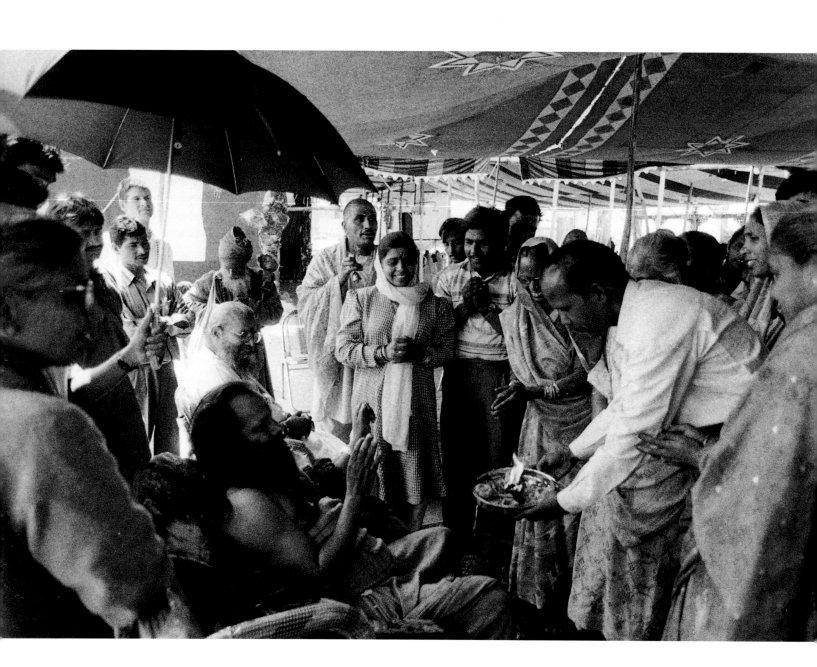

We have come from the cosmic senses and we had to discover the route of the seed to the plant to the tree in order to realize that we have a mind, we have consciousness, and we have being. To know the cycle of our being is to know the truth of being and our relationship to the whole.

In India we do not refer to *citta* as the mind, because *citta* is more than what the West refers to as consciousness. *Citta* is divided into three parts. We refer to these parts as *sat*, which means truth; *raj* means excellence; and together they are *tam*, the energy needed to transcend. These three aspects of *citta* are also represented by the three important deities: Brahma, Shiva, and Vishnu. Brahma is creation and truth, Vishnu is the preserver of creation, and when the two energies come together equally, this is Shiva. Shiva is the symbol of destruction and transcendence.

If you can separate yourself from your body and your mind and realize that you are that being, everything will be unveiled. You are at one with the whole. Free yourself from consciousness by holding fast to your *samskaras*. *Samskara* means the memory of the thousands and millions of years of your past; that is where you find yourself. Unveil everything, and the being you are then becomes at one with the whole.

Samadhi means oneness to the Self; beyond detachment. The body becomes the universe and we become the masters. The road to *samadhi* leads to total freedom, to think and observe your being. *Samadhi* is a silence totally within oneself, showing us that we have a destination in the spiritual world. To reach the end of *samadhi* is the meaning of life; to cross the barrier of death and time and existence. We are born into silence and are returned to silence. When you enter yourself into *samadhi*, everything becomes open to you; all doubts and curiosities are gone. You yourself are the universe once you cross the barrier of the ego by freeing yourself from the desires of attachment.

The meaning of life is that the basic ground of being is truth. We are the truth because we have no more mystery; we are born and we die. Dying is a truth; life is a truth. Religion is not a truth, because to explain the truth is not the truth; it is only knowledge. Everything comes out into the truth and everything will disappear into the truth; the only thing that remains is *santi,*[1] *santi, santi.*"

1 Inner peace.

Prem Puri Baba

B. RAJASTHAN

Prem Puri Baba was a mechanical engineer with a family of four before becoming a *sadhu* in 1986. Surrendering everything he owned and loved to devote himself to God, Puri Babaji decided to take a more extreme and selfless austerity: *mauna vrata*, the vow of silence. The vow of silence he took was for ten years. Having completed eight years, living mainly on rice and curd, his vow ends at the Kumbha Mela in Allahabad on January 14, 2001. My questions were answered in chalk on his slate-board and translated from Hindi by an Indian medical doctor. It was Puri Babaji's ninth day of fasting as part of a *puja*[1] to the Goddess Durga.[2]

The day after his portrait was photographed, Puri Babaji arrived with his head shaved. He explained, using his slate, that his hair was shaved off in a single piece and thrown into the River Ganges at a dawn ceremony as an offering. He expressed that the experience of silence was God's gift to him.

"Faith is understanding yourself and knowing your path. Faith is to believe in God. There are many ways to reach God, but the easiest path is by chanting and praying. You go within yourself; you forget everything material. You have to understand yourself completely, the internal and the external. People know about the body and the senses, but they forget the soul. Truth is knowing where we come from and where we have to go."

Puri Babaji quoted Sri Ramana Maharshi:

Silence is so potent. Silence is the loudest form of prayer.

1   Ceremonial offering of worship.
2   The consort to Shiva.

Raj Kumar Anat Prasad Singh

B. BIHAR

The last in a long succession of kings, Raj[1] Kumar Anat Prasad Singh was born into a life of material wealth and influence. Through a spiritual awakening in his early thirties, he turned away from materialism to lead a renounced life. Raj Kumar does not engage in business, wears simple robes, and occupies humble quarters within the grounds of the large family temple in Vrindavan. As president of the temple, he conducts the daily ritual of devotional prayers and has opened its doors to those on a pilgrimage through the holy city.

"The title of king gets passed down from generation to generation, but kingships have now finished in India. I was born a king and in many ways my life was better than my father's, because I had more time on my hands. He was Raja Kumar Sachiananda Prasad Singh, and my grandfather was Raja Rishish Raghunanda Prasad Singh, Knight of Mungar in Bihar.

I started life eating with a golden spoon. I lived in a palace and I had twenty of my own servants. Krishna had given me everything, without any effort from me. I put this down to my past *samskaras*. I must have done something right in my past life to have it so easy this time. When I went to school, and later to college, many people wanted to befriend me because I had everything I desired. I had eight personal cars, including a Rolls-Royce, which I changed every year for a new one. When I went to Diamond Jubilee College, which belonged to my family, I was above the principal. He would ask me what to do, and my professors took great care of my needs. I graduated with a Bachelor of Science degree and took over the family businesses. It was very difficult for me to understand the material world. I just enjoyed it and made more business. With all my wealth and enjoyment, I did not feel deeply satisfied. I looked at my elders and their spiritual practices to which I was connected, being president of our family temple. They all looked very happy, so I began to question what I was doing.

One day I decided that I was going to give up all my business activities and not do anything except to start searching for divine love. That was twenty years ago. I found it in my spiritual master, Sri Sri Radha Govind Das Babaji Maharaj. When I met my master, I was immediately taken by his behavior, by his softness and his love. I surrendered completely and faith took hold of me. My master said he saw the day when I would preach to people on the other side of the world using love, and that they would love me. I told him no, that I had no capacity for anything like that, because I was very poor in my spiritual life. He gave me his mercy and showed me the path of understanding.

My master sent me to meet His Divine Grace Swami Prabhupada. Swami asked me who I was and when I told him, he embraced me and said that he and my grandfather had been good friends. Swami Prabhupada gave me guidelines. When I told him what I was doing in my life, with my many business duties to take care of, he asked me why I was wasting my time. Swami reminded me that my grandfather had managed his duties and still maintained a sincerely devoted spiritual life. That shocked me, and my life changed even more toward the path of devotion.

Reality is when you understand the heart. We are not just a body; we are more than the body. I am living in this house, but I am not this house. Similarly, we are living in this body — it is like a house — but we are not this body. Our existence is separate. When someone dies, we say they are no more, but who is no more? Our existence is not the external body. You are more than the body. Your soul lives in this body and it simply moves on. The soul comes from Super Soul. We come from there and we have to return there. The true meaning of spirituality is this relationship to Super Soul.

I went to South America in 1995 by invitation and in Colombia I started to preach to the people. They loved me so much and I realized it was time to take *sannyasa*.[2] I went to Miami in 1996 to take my vows and that experience changed my life forever. I did not become a *sannyasin*[3] to build big ashrams, because I had many ashrams before. I have enjoyed airconditioned rooms before, so I have no desire for that either. Now I serve humanity, by giving service to people from my heart, because I understand that is my real duty in this life."

1 King.
2 Initiation into the renounced order of life.
3 One who has taken the vow of renunciation.

Syeed Mumtaz Husin

B. MADHYA PRADESH

Syeed Mumtaz Husin is a devout Muslim, a merchant, an astrologer, and the father of seven, who lives behind the Taj Mahal in Agra. He answers the call for *salah*, the obligatory prayer, five times every day of his life. The ritualistic performance of *salah* is prescribed to all Muslim males from the age of seven.

"Belief is trusting only one power, which is Allah or God. We use a different name, but God is one superior power. To respect His name, we should do what has been explained to us in the Koran and other holy books. As human beings we are brothers all over the world. God has sent messengers to explain to us the right and the wrong way. The messengers were called prophets, and God said Mohammed would be the last prophet that He would send us and we should listen to his instructions. Mohammed said there is no partner to God; He is only One and He is alone. The prophet said: '*La'ilaha'illa'Llah*, there is no god but God.' The meaning of being a Muslim is that we believe in God.

A man's heart is like a mirror and it shows on his face. If you explain yourself to someone and you are honest, then they will see it on your face; but if there is dishonesty, then the expression on the face will be different. Allah said that we should have respect for His messengers and for every person on earth, no matter what color their skin or whatever their religion. Allah said: 'All are equal.'

As a Muslim I must pray five times a day at the mosque, but first I have to prepare myself. I wake up early in the morning, at about 4.30, and begin my wash. Three times I wash my hands, and three times I wash my mouth and in my nose and my face completely. Then three times I wash my arms; first the right and then the left, right down to my feet. Everything must be washed three times; only then are you completely clean for prayer. It is most important that your clothes are clean and that no dirt touches your body when you go for morning worship.

The morning prayer is the most important one. The first prayer is the gift of God. Twice we pray in the afternoon, and then there is the sunset prayer and the last prayer for the day, when it is night time. The Koran says that when you go to God your flesh is not there, only your soul. The body is nothing. Only the soul has power, like electricity. When you switch it off, there is no light without power. This light, which is the soul, goes to God. The soul does not come back. There is only one life and then it is finished until the end of the world, the final judgment. Heaven is like a very beautiful garden as it is explained in the books, a place for good people, and hell is a place of fire and snakes. Love is a very great thing and does not depend on where you are from, or who you are, or how much money you have. Love comes from the heart and if your heart is clean, then your life is true.

God is like a gardener with so many different flowers in His garden. Some are good-smelling flowers and some are not, and some have beautiful colors. God, as the gardener, gives water equally to the plants. He never separates the water between the good- and bad-smelling plants or those with colors and those with none. God is also like the big gardener for all human beings. He gives His love like water, and every person receives His love equally. We should read the books that He has sent us. People should take the time to read the Holy Koran and it may help them to understand life better."

On the peak of the white snow mountains in the East

a white cloud seems to be rising towards the sky.

At the instance of beholding it, I remember my teacher

and, pondering over his kindness, faith stirs in me.

TIBETAN SONG OF THE EASTERN SNOW MOUNTAIN

His Holiness the Dalai Lama Tenzin Gyatso

In the month of March each year, His Holiness the Dalai Lama Tenzin Gyatso, the Fourteenth Dalai Lama, gives his annual private audiences and general public lectures at his temple in McLeod Ganj. His Holiness, as spiritual and political leader of Tibet, has resided in McLeod Ganj, near Dharamsala, for most of his self-imposed exile from Tibet in 1959. Although His Holiness was not interviewed for this book, I did photograph him amid tight security as he greeted members of the audience who attended his lecture and have included this extract from a speech.

"My general belief is something quite simple. All sentient beings, particularly human beings, no matter whether they are educated or uneducated, rich or poor, easterners or westerners, believers or non-believers, each one wants happiness and does not want suffering. This is the nature of all sentient beings. I believe happiness comes from happiness. Happiness cannot come from hatred or anger. Through kindness, whether at our own level or at the national or international level, through mutual understanding, and through mutual respect we will get peace, we will get happiness, and we will get genuine satisfaction. It is very difficult to achieve peace and harmony through competition and hatred, so the practice of kindness is very, very important and very, very valuable in human society. Here we don't need a deeper philosophy, we don't need monasteries, we don't need temples, we don't need images and so on, we don't need gods — we can simply practice kindness. So try to become a good human being. By a good human being, I mean a warm-hearted person."

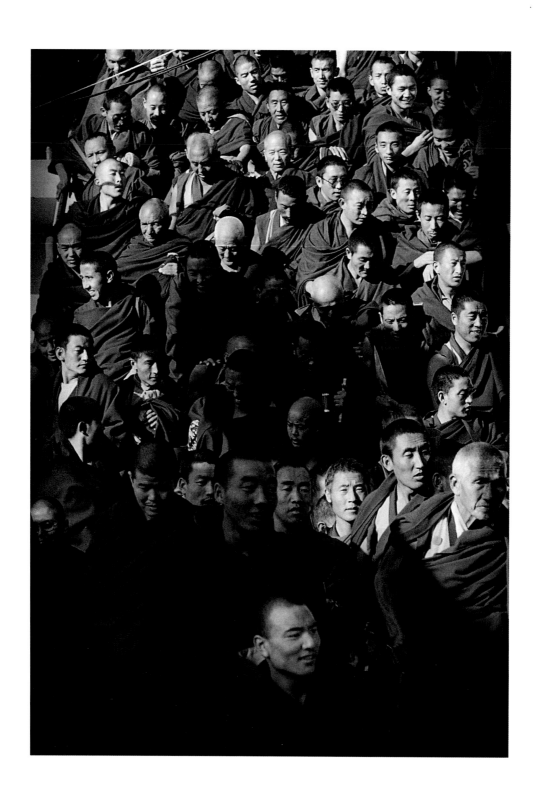

Shanti Bala

B. BIHAR

Born a Roman Catholic, Shanti Bala's parents and grandparents were all Catholics. She has attended the Sunday service at the St. John's Church in the Wilderness for many years, which is close to her home in Forsyth Ganj, near Dharamsala.

"Being a Christian, I have realized my faith so many times. I have called to God and whenever I call, under any circumstances, I am helped by all His means; mentally, spiritually, and physically. Even when I call for help for other people, they have been healed with prayer. I have seen healing come with my own eyes. I have the most faith in Mother Mary. I go through Mary to Jesus Christ and then to God. I am here today because it is God's plan; about tomorrow, I cannot say. It is His wish and I am prepared if He takes me. I am ready to go whenever He calls.

From morning to evening I work for the nation, but in the evening I find nothing in my life unless I thank God for everything that happens every day. Then I say 'Take me into Your lap' and I go peacefully to sleep. If the sunrise comes the next day, then it is because of His great mercy that He is giving me another day. My connection to God is through prayer. Early in the morning I remember Him, and in the evenings and before and after meals and on Sundays at the Church. I have my own prayer that I learnt in my childhood and I am continuing it today. Praying helps me to concentrate and know that God will help by all His means. In the Roman Catholic Church we have a rosary to help us. Rosary is a prayer. There are ten beads on a string that you count five times. When one circle is over, that is one completed rosary. I do that in the evenings but especially in the months of May and October, when I do it without fail.

Truth is nature and it is created by God because of His goodness. His creation is in even the smallest creatures. In Hindi there is a saying which means 'the world is yours but your soul belongs to God.'"

THOMPSON-NICOLA REGIONAL DISTRICT LIBRARY SYSTEM

Braja Raj Khalsa Sukh Dev Das Kathiya Baba

B. BANKS OF THE GANGES SOMEWHERE

Braja Raj Khalsa Sukh Dev Das Kathiya Baba is well known and respected among the Kathiya Babas because he has been wearing his wooden *langoti* for more than two periods. Each mandatory period is twelve years. On our second meeting, I witnessed Kathiya Babaji sitting in a "circle of fire." The "fire" for this austerity was produced by the intense heat of smoldering heaps of cow dung formed into a circle. He was naked except for his *langoti* and completely covered in ash, as he sat chanting in the midday sun for more than two hours. The temperature in Haridwar that day was 42° Celsius in the shade.

"When I was a boy I asked my father what I should do with my life. He said: 'Go and live on the banks of the Ganga and she will teach you everything you need to know about the cycles of life.' So that is exactly what I did.

Faith means to enjoy, and I am enjoying the occurrence of my faith. It is a state of boundlessness. Faith is the only path and it is the only way. People serve the Superlative, which is the way I say God, according to their ability as they become enlightened. There are no words to describe the Superlative. He is unpronounceable. He is more like pure sound, like the sound of the '*Om.*' The sound of creation is indescribable. Faith is the stirring of consciousness.

The Kathiya Babas serve and worship the Superlative. To be a Kathiya is a special style of behavior which is a statement and an expression of our devotion. We are simply here together at the Kumbh to perform service and nothing else. For us there is no difference in our devotion between night and day; it never stops. Time is a system in nature that has nothing really to do with mankind. There are many levels to living life, but each new level depends on faith and realization. There is knowledge available, but you have to want to follow it. What is the value of knowledge if it is not realized and not practiced? It has no value. With the knowledge I have, there is no confusion. I have killed off all the aspects of myself known as 'the wrong universal language.'

Truth is in your actions. Truth is not a word for me until it has been acted. My actions are an example of my faith, and obediency is one of our main tasks. Obediency is humility, and I have never questioned this. Just sitting in this chair, I am behaving in service, realizing and surrendering. My whole realization is through my faith. You cannot define truth; you have to realize it. True consciousness is what you gain from having a spiritual practice. Consciousness makes you sensitive, and achieving the sense, that is *samadhi*. *Samadhi* is the knowledge of creation."

Animosity does not
eradicate animosity.
Only by loving kindness
is animosity dissolved.
This law is ancient
and eternal.

THE BUDDHA

Pramod Goswami

B. BENGAL

While studying for a Bachelor of Commerce degree, Pramod Goswami was afflicted with typhoid which caused his blindness. He works as a begging musician on the banks of the River Ganges in Rishikesh, with the support of his wife and baby.

"I play my harmonium and sing my mantra to God. My devotion is to God. I sing my *sadhana*,[1] the Mahamantra, the great mantra of deliverance:

Hare Krishna Hare Krishna Krishna Krishna Hare Hare

Hare Rama Hare Rama Rama Rama Hare Hare

This is the sixteen-syllable mantra which salutes the supreme Lord Krishna and which will purify and deliver me across the *'ocean of samsara.'*[2] Now, for me, my whole life is dependent on the generosity of the devotees of God. True feeling for God is love."

1 Spiritual practice.
2 Realms of continuous rebirth in delusion.

Lobsang Gawa

B. TIBET

Lobsang Gawa is a monk and a secretary at the Namgyal Tibetan Buddhist Monastery at McLeod Ganj, where His Holiness the Dalai Lama Tenzin Gyatso conducts his annual public lectures. He yearns to return to his native Tibet from which he escaped as a boy after the Chinese invasion in 1959.

"For me, spirituality and religion are the one thing, which is about compassion. As a Tibetan Buddhist, I am mainly concerned with the practice of compassion.

I was born in Tibet, and when I was a boy it was not possible to practice any faith. Nothing was allowed under the Chinese occupation. In Tibetan culture and in my family, we always spoke about the practice of Buddhism. We wanted to circumambulate our temples but it was prohibited by the Chinese for us to do that. Still, we did it; we practiced our faith. They could never stop us and it gave me strong impressions. My grandmother was my spiritual teacher. When I was a boy, she taught me not to harm even an insect; she taught me everything. My grandmother took me to circumambulate the temples, but we had to be very careful. We had to make a big circle around the temples because if the Chinese saw us … It was not allowed.

And you see, now I am a monk, from my strong childhood impressions. I follow the teachings of Buddha, and the main teaching is about compassion. There is not even enough time in this life for all the teachings of the Buddha. We have to work hard at spiritual development and all things will come. Love is precious."

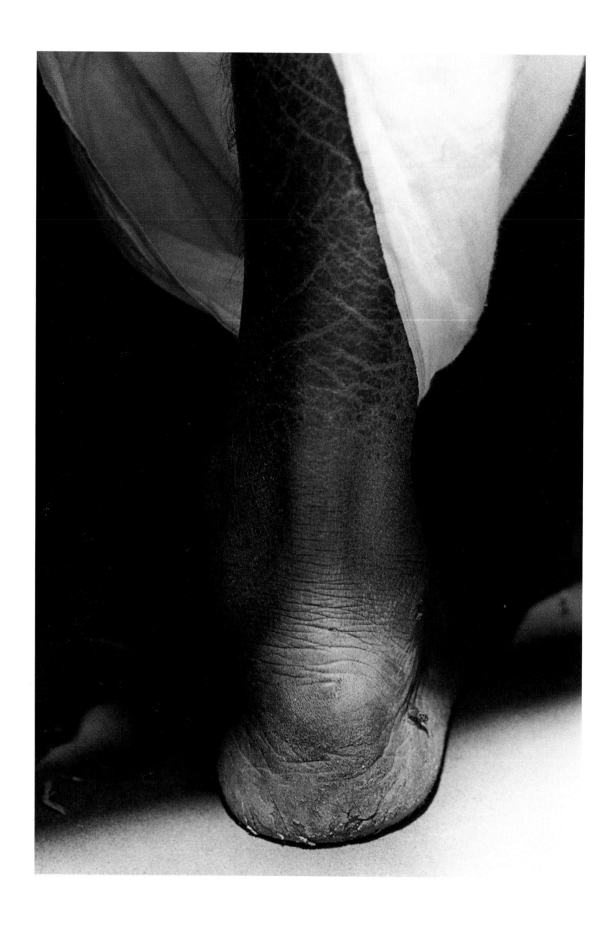

Detachment is not indifference.

It is the prerequisite for effective involvement.

Often what we think is best for others is

distorted by our attachment to our opinions:

we want others to be happy in the way

we think they should be happy.

It is only when we want nothing

for ourselves that we are able

to see clearly into others' needs

and understand how to serve them.

MAHATMA GANDHI

Gopi Giri Baba

B. HIMACHAL PRADESH

Gopi Giri Baba is also known as Nepali Baba, because he has lived alone in the ice caves of the Himalaya in Nepal for the past twenty-four years. He is rarely seen anywhere in India except at a Kumbha Mela, and then only on the auspicious bathing days. People who have befriended him say that he lives "scientifically" on yoga and very little food. Local villagers leave wheat and rice near his cave from time to time. They say he is "God's child" and that it is God who keeps him alive.

Giri Babaji would not be interviewed or photographed until he had seen my right hand. After looking at it for a minute or two, he smiled and slowly nodded. When I later questioned the medical doctor who acted as our interpreter, he said that Giri Babaji wanted to establish whether or not I had lived a previous life in India. The doctor added that had I not, my request for an interview would not have been successful.

Q. *What is your connection to God?*
A. What is true is that if you pray to God, you automatically get the connection. God has a connection with me. I am too humble to say I have a connection to God. I do not know Him; He only knows me.

Q. *What is truth?*
A. God is truth. That is God.

Q. *What is* samadhi?
A. I can say nothing of *samadhi.*

Q. *What are your religious practices?*
A. I only do Tantric *japa.*[1] I chant my mantra continuously to reach the "illuminated point," which is like a star in the sky.

Q. *What is the purpose of your life?*
A. To meet God — nothing else.

Q. *What is reality, and is this real?*
A. This is real; thinking is not real.

Q. *What is time?*
A. Not fixed.

Q. *What is the meaning of this life?*
A. We were sent for and we surrendered, one by one. Nobody called anybody; you came, we came, and we sat here. This was decided already, this was decided before — it became; we did nothing.

Q. *What is it to surrender to God?*
A. Whatever He says I should do or wherever I should go. I have surrendered everything to God.

Q. *What is love?*
A. God's name is love.

1 The repetitive recital of a mantra or holy name.

Hafiz Jafir Ahamad

B. UTTAR PRADESH

Hafiz Jafir Ahamad is the *imam* of Chotta Bazaar Masjid in Agra. He was only willing to discuss aspects of Islam, and to be photographed, with the blessing of the *mufti*. Hafiz added that the beard is symbolically important to Muslim male culture, as it commands respect and gives beauty to the face.

"Faith, for me, is having confidence in Allah. We should always remember Him, because if we forget Him then He will not help us. Allah gives me orders and I pass those orders to the people of my mosque. If they accept those orders from Allah, then He will be pleased; but if not, those people cannot be helped. Our faith only accepts the orders of Allah. Prayer is important to help us keep our faith. In prayer, people often demand different desires like physical health or wealth. Allah knows our desires, so instead we should ask for His grace.

Morning prayer is like a meditation and the first prayer is called *salat as-subh* and begins at 5.20 a.m. If the time has passed and a person is late, then they will not be accepted. They will have to pray another time. *Salat az-zuhr* is the second prayer at 12.30 p.m. where people pray for natural happiness; if you get happiness, then you can give it to others. *Salat al-asr* is at 5.30 p.m. This is the time to pray for love and progress and purity and trueness. *Salat al-maghrib* is at 6.50 p.m. and in this prayer, one applies to Allah to give happiness to the whole world. *Salat al-isha* is the last prayer and begins at 8.50 p.m. It is a time to remember Allah and to ask for His mercy. If you pray five times a day at the mosque, this will make Allah happy; and if you pray from the heart, then Allah will be near you. If you have fine clothes, He will not notice that; it is the heart and soul of a man that is important. The aim of my work as a priest is not for money, it is for my inner peace. Allah gave me knowledge, and I share that knowledge with the people, from house to house.

Our first duty as Muslims is to speak the truth because, through truth, love will automatically grow. If we have divine love, then people will come closer and respect us and in turn we will respect them. We should give love everywhere — to animals, to plants, and to humans alike, because every living thing needs love. Where there is love, there is Allah. Love is everything, and without love nobody can find the path to Allah. With love you will never be worried and success will come to your life. A real Muslim does good in his community and is always ready for service and cooperation. Day or night, he must be ready to help others.

Allah gave us this body for good actions, hands to do good, and a mouth for speaking sweetly. When the world finishes, only Allah will be left, because He is our creator. The real judgment will come only after our death. If your actions were good, then you will benefit in your future life. All good karma stays in your heart. Allah will decide the balance between good and bad. Good souls will be sent by Him to a new world which will be a heavenly place.

Truth is God's gift, but not everybody has this. Allah controls everything, so those who believe and who have confidence in Him will grow. If He orders that we do good deeds, then we will do them. If you do good in this world in your life, then Allah will give you His grace. Whatever you have extra of or to excess, it is your duty to share. If the needy come to you for food or shelter or clothing and you have extra, then it must be shared. Honest people keep their donations to the needy secret. People should give without talking about it; that is real kindness and Allah knows. He is always watching."[1]

---

1   English–Urdu conversation translated by Sunhari Lal Kaith.

Shyam Sandar Das Parivrajak

B. TARANTO, ITALY

Shyam Sandar Das Parivrajak has lived continuously in India for the past six years. He wears white *sannyasi* robes and walks barefoot. He is a scholar and a freelance writer who speaks fluent Hindi. Shyam leads a deeply ascetic life, spending each day engaged in his devotional practices. These include chanting and walking the route of *parikrama*, a sacred path around the outer perimeter of the city of Vrindavan. Shyam chooses to live in Vrindavan because it is only in such a holy city that he feels comfortable living his austere life.

"The basic truths are found in the Vedanta,[1] written by the great Sankaracarya a thousand years ago. He was one of the greatest reformers of India and his influence spread far and wide. Sankara re-established the Vedas[2] in India and one basic truth that he established was that we are spirit and not matter. That we are not flesh and blood should be clear to everyone, to Christians and Muslims alike. How can I say I have a soul? We cannot possess a soul, because we *are* the soul and we are the 'experiencers.' We have to make an experience of it because we are of a different nature. If we are the soul, then what is our position as such? We are helped by the saints and they have informed us that we are the servants of God. This is like a key to enter into a higher understanding. We are the servants and not the masters; we are spirit. If someone understands that fully, then they can get very close to God.

It is important to have some point of reference in life. From youth to old age, the soul is continuously passing through the body. The body is changing, but your being is not changing. From birth, you live your whole life in your body. When the body is no longer habitable, then you have to leave the body and with that you will have to leave your own attachments to the body. This point about reincarnation is very important to understand. You have to put aside everything, including the body which is the object we are attached to the most. Sometimes we say that we are attached to our family or to our society or to the earth, but in reality we are simply attached to our body. Everything else is just an extended idea.

In this world, we are an esoteric concept, we are different from our names. You could call anything by any name; we are the ones who have given them their names. We are different from our bodies. Krishna is no different from his body, but then Krishna is not made of material elements but completely of spiritual elements. Even Krishna's famous 'rasa[3] lila,' the *rasa* dance in Vrindavan, was not a material affair. On the outside it looked like he was enjoying himself with the *gopis*[4] in the dead of night in the autumn season, which is so beautiful in India. People look at that and question why they should lead renounced lives if Krishna behaved that way; but they were not material beings, they were transcendental beings. Transcendental means beyond the limitations of time and space. What is time? Time is a spiritual concept, but we in the West have killed the concept of time. Time is eternal but we do not use our time properly. We are all just wasting time. We think we have enough time, but we should remember that time does not come back, so we should value our single instinct; that our mission be fulfilled. People say that there are so many missions in the world. Every single human entity has a mission, the mission of their own life. It is not so much whether you achieve perfection or not, but the desire to achieve perfection is a glorious attempt. My guru used to say: 'In a man, ideal is all.'

Faith is a subtle element linking us to the spiritual world. We have no information about the spiritual world, so what makes us convinced is faith. Faith means a link, and if you want to communicate with the spiritual world, you need a medium. This is not to be found in the material world, so we need a fine element from the spiritual world. Everyone speaks about happiness, and when everyone speaks about something, it is often because it is important. Happiness is very important for all of us and yet happiness is something that, when you speak about it, practically nothing can be said. It is an experience. We have to make an experience of happiness. Sometimes people are frightened by religious faith, because all religions promise happiness and people pursue that happiness along certain paths but they cannot find it. The fault is not with the religion or the path; most of the time, the problem is with us. Happiness lies within, not without. So if we remember this, then we will live more harmoniously.

In society these days, the media controls people. I think everyone is aware of that, but people seem to like being controlled. Westerners are so stubborn about not accepting the idea of a guru, yet they will accept the control of the media. Everyone goes to school and has a teacher. If you want a driver's licence you will need a teacher, and if you want a university degree you will need the help of professors — so why not accept, a guru, a teacher? Unfortunately, this is the time of 'Kali-yuga,' the 'age of quarrel and suspicion.' If you have suspicion, you cannot do anything. If you suspect someone, your relationship is suspended. In a guru–disciple relationship there should be some affection, some love, because it is that kind of transaction. Just as there is nothing wrong with money; it is the way you use it that creates good or bad. What is wrong with a knife? A knife can cut bread or it can cut a throat, it all depends on how you use it. Of course, the guru must be qualified and he must have experience that he can share with others. Not a dry thing, not parrot-like knowledge from a book. Books will always be there. The guru should be a personification of those books. The idea of a guru is easily accepted in India for one reason: people understand that the guru is for their good. There is no loss in the exchange between the guru and the disciple. The word 'guru' means teacher, and if the teacher is genuine and sincere, then no-one will have to be saved from exploitation. When one accepts a guru, they are accepting a friend who is going to unveil for them the mysteries of spiritual knowledge.

If you want to please God, you will have to serve God. We want to achieve and we want to take, but without establishing a relationship or doing service to God. When we love God, we love everything else; it is not a separate affair. It is not that we love God, and that means religious practice and neglect of everything else. If you take the idea of God-realization, then within God, the self is included. The idea is that if you can understand God, you can understand yourself. Just like within one million dollars, you also have one thousand dollars; you don't need to separate them. There is only one reality and that is God. We are all parts of Him, but this is not meant in a mathematical way; we share the same nature as God. We are filled with knowledge; we only have to rediscover it. We are meant for happiness, not suffering. The German philosopher Hegel said: 'Reality is by itself and for itself.' Reality alone — who is that reality? God. God is reality and it is by itself. It does not need any support. It does not need to be demonstrated beyond reality, which does not need any demonstration. People ask, 'What is God?' People try to grasp it, but this is not possible; it is to be achieved, but it is inconceivable. That is the only reality. Our goal in life is to consciously play a part, because unconsciously we are there anyway. To play a part consciously is our duty and our challenge if we would like to accept it.

Swami Prabhupada, the founder of the Hare Krishna movement, used to say, 'Chant Hare Krishna and be happy.' In a general way this was true. We should try to have a practice of devotion, to be God-conscious, and try to be happy with that. God loves us so much, even if we don't know it. He is also advising us to be happy with our spiritual practices, which are actions inherently filled with bliss. How do we know that? We have to experience it, you have to try it — otherwise, whatever we say or do will

amount to nothing. 'The proof is in the pudding,' as they say. We should make an experience of it and if the experience is not satisfactory, then we can always turn to the material life. We are so expert at doing that anyway. We always find some pretext to turn to a material life, so it is not a new concept for us, but the spiritual life is like a new experience. It is worth trying, and we are not the losers; the only consideration is that we have to go deep. You have to dive deep. It is one thing to get your toes wet at the seaside, but if you dive in, only then can you understand the mystery of the ocean. In the same way, you can be on the surface of realization, or you can accept systems that allow you to go down to a deep level. Again, it is up to you. No-one should be forced. We are not God, but we can enjoy a high position, like a servant of God. All Vaisnavas are called *das*, which means servant.

It does not matter how much philosophy you can digest. Philosophy is called the intellect, but we have to consider other factors about this life. If someone wants to find the highest achievement, and this is the desire for God, one has to come to India. Westerners should not become envious at this point. India is called *punya bhumi*, the 'land of virtue' where our karma — the law of action and reaction — must finish. This is not to be seen in black and white; this is a devotional law. We do things and can expect some results. If that is true on a material level, then it must be true in the spiritual also. It is a good start if someone can approach India through the scriptures, because, after all, if we want to know the truth, we will need some help. We should be humble enough to accept truth from others. On our journey everything will become lighter. It is like traveling with a companion — the journey is somehow easier. The spiritual world is not a place for boredom or for boring oneself. We are eternally fresh — the soul is eternal. That is such important knowledge of the soul, and people would get much strength in their lives by understanding that. There is the body, the mind, and spirit — soul. You are the soul and whatever happens to one here is not really happening, it is just a material circumstance. The soul cannot be cut into pieces; it cannot be moistened by water or burnt with fire. It is just like when one is wearing old, worn-out clothes; at a certain point you throw them away and put on new clothes. In the same way, when your body becomes consumed, it means it is no longer habitable and the house of your soul must be left. Our duty is to maintain the body, because the body does not really belong to us. The body is like a vehicle and when the moment of death comes, we do not want to leave the vehicle because we have become very much attached to it. Hindu and Buddhist philosophy comes to our help by telling us to 'become detached.' Self-realization should not wait for us; we should move toward self-realization.

To acquire knowledge, four factors are necessary. The first is *sadhu*, the saints who are experiencing the bliss of spiritual life. Then *sastra*, which means where that experience is recorded faithfully. Guru is the most brilliant example among the *sadhus*, without the limitation of age. *Citta* is the most important of all — it means heart. You can have *sadhus* and *sastra* and the guru, but unless your heart confirms, nothing will work. This knowledge you can experience directly in the heart and no-one can take it away from you. The experience you have made will become yours permanently, and it is sacred and mysterious. It will defend you. It will be your permanent support, your heritage, and it is important to have that kind of support in life. You just have to be humble enough to read the signs that the Lord is continually sending us. We are full of knowledge, we only have to rediscover it. In all religions, it is not that one scripture will give you something more than another; it depends only on your eyes. If your eyes are developed, then you will find your treasure right there in front of you.

In reality, anyone can turn to a sentient life. It can be seen as a duty, that everyone should try to lead a dignified life. A sentient life does not mean that one has to renounce their duties in the world. One can keep doing whatever one is doing: study, marriage, work, and living in society. The more honest seeker will go deeper and deeper, and in doing so eliminate unnecessary aspects of themselves. My guru used to say: 'Elimination of something old and acceptance of something new.' We are always the students, not the teachers, so spread the news that we are in a land that is foreign to us. We have nothing to do with the material world. This world is like a foreign land; we suffer because we don't know the language or the customs. We wander here and there, trying to do so many things and collecting so much knowledge and so many possessions, but we forget to turn our attention to our Father who gave us everything. When we approach Him, we don't know what to say, we don't know how to ask. The highest request is no request. When your desires become zero without any material desires — neither physical nor intellectual desires — then, and only from that stage, can pure devotion begin.

Austerities are a duty for human beings. What it really means is to understand our true nature. There are many different types of austerities of the mind and body. Austerities of the body include showing respect to others or prostrating oneself before entering a temple. Another austerity of the body is to get up early every morning. All the Vedic scriptures talk about rising early for the 'morning bath.' This is the period for a few hours before sunrise that has a special energy which is so conducive to meditation and prayer. In the material world this is a time to be sleeping soundly, but the more enlightened ones will wake up.

As a principle, it is not good to advertise one's spiritual practice to others, because *bhajan* means secret. It is your secret with Him. Certain things can, however, be said without any harm. In general for our times, the chanting of the names of God is especially recommended. This is not a whimsical idea; it is recognized as the highest and the easiest way, but because it is the easiest, people don't want to take it seriously. They prefer the hardest and most complicated methods of meditation. The chanting of the holy name is a sacrifice in this age. People want to know about love, but first they should know that love means to sacrifice. Love is based on sacrifice, and so unless there is a sacrifice, love will not be produced. That is sacrifice in this age, the chanting of the holy name. You receive the *japa* or mantra from your guru and you faithfully chant the mantra. The potency of the guru is transmitted into the mantra and, if you practice that, you will achieve the realization that your guru has. Caitanya Mahaprabhu inaugurated the chanting of the names of God in his age. That is why he was so prominent. He said, 'One should be more humble than a blade of grass.' My opinion is not that he woke up one morning with the idea of writing a poem. No, he actually saw the world like that — he had a vision."

1   Philosophy derived from the Upanishads, a scriptural authority of Hinduism.
2   A collection of the oldest known scriptures, dating to 2000 BC.
3   The essence of spiritual enjoyment.
4   Cowherd girls.

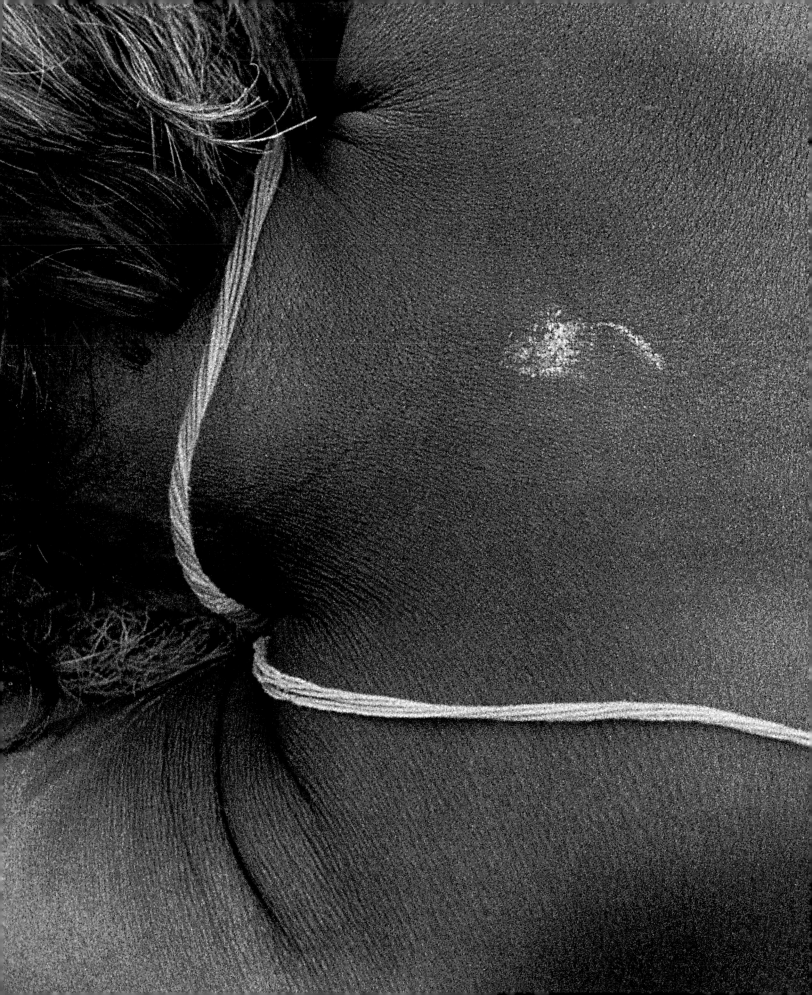

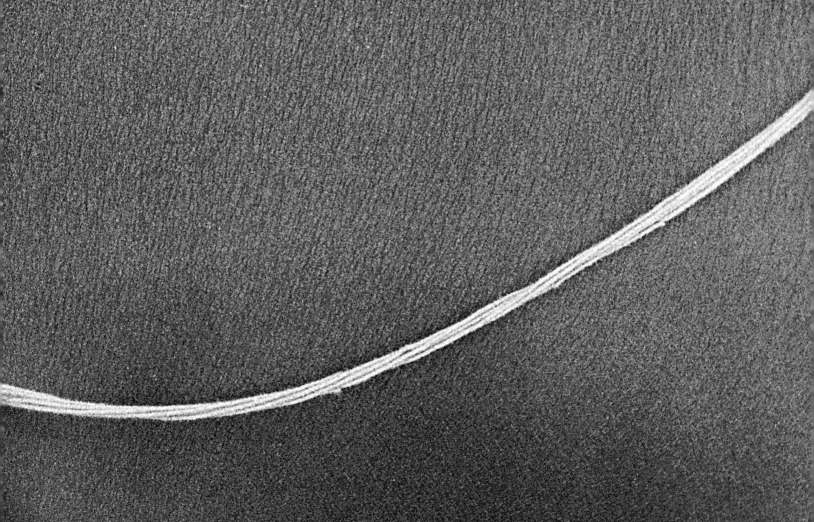

When one sees Eternity in things that pass away

and Infinity in finite things, then one has pure knowledge.

BHAGAVAD-GITA

Swami Premananda Baba

B. UTTAR PRADESH

Swami Premananda Baba has lived in Vrindavan, one of the holiest cities in India, for sixty-four years. In the twilight of his devout life, he happily contemplates his inexorable passing, which he refers to as "the moment of ultimate happiness." It is said that Yama, the Lord of Death, loses claim to the souls of those devotees who leave their bodies in Vrindavan.

"God has not forgotten us; we have forgotten God. If God forgot us for even a single second, our existence would come to an end. It is He who is present from top to toe, in every impulse, in every expression, and in every action. Faith is what you feel. It is your relationship with God. If you feel that relationship, then faith and love will come. We have not come here of our own accord — we were impelled to come here. A child does not need to be taught to love its mother or father. The child feels their love; no injection of faith is required. Once you come to know your relationship with God, then you will have achieved everything. You will have no need ever to leave that path of devotion. Faith and happiness are not at the end of the path, but along the path. That journey, if compared to all other journeys, is not the same if their completion is only at the end: home sweet home. This is a misunderstanding. Happiness begins with you, wherever you are, in whatever conditions or country or circumstances. Your happiness lies within you, not without; it is a state of mind.

Truth is the name of truth. The thing that exists is truth. That exists not today, not tomorrow and not yesterday, but since existence itself. That which cannot be described by anyone, that is truth. In the beginning there was the world, the same world that is moving us around, that pervades. When all these visible forms have been dissolved and disappear, even then it will remain. It was, it is, and it will be. That is truth. Unless you know the truth, you can never be free from the vortex of birth and death and from all the pain and suffering and misery in this world. Socrates taught us to know this truth. In his time there were so many deities, gods, and goddesses, but Socrates stood up and said: 'Behind all these forms, there is only one truth.' For that, Socrates drank the cup of poison but he never gave up his view. Today Socrates is worshiped. All the religions and all their texts say: 'Know thyself.' This is the seed of knowledge, and without this, nothing will sprout.

The purpose of your life is to know yourself and to attain happiness and bliss. For everlasting happiness, the place is not important. You need not look for external help, because it is all within you. You only have to change the direction of your mind. Once you put yourself in the right direction, you are sure to realize the goal of understanding. The mind that is not clear will need to be purified. For purification, every single word and every little act will make a difference. You will have to be very careful with your thinking and your speaking and your actions. Not only that, but also through the five senses. At present, our knowledge is limited to what we perceive with these five senses. It is the senses that can mislead us and we will have to learn to keep them under control. They are like horses that have to be harnessed. These five senses of knowledge draw us in different directions and, if caught in their tentacles, one can never be satisfied.

Everyone runs after happiness. One spends a lifetime achieving real happiness, but in fact it is all a mirror to God. All one has to do is to turn in the other direction. Kindness and love are the opposite sides of the same coin. Where you find kindness, you find love. Love is something that does not cost a thing. Love is natural to us; you only have to realize the relationship between the Divine and the

follower. It is a relationship that you must know so as to understand that we are part of the whole. If you belong to a particular religious group, you are following a path where a long succession of saints have worshiped. If you follow that way, at least it is a safer way, instead of trying to follow blindly. That can only lead to self-doubt, which is a destroyer of faith and love. The moment that doubt enters your mind, your peace and happiness will disappear. Tolstoy wrote a book entitled *How Much Land Does a Man Require?* The land symbolizes all the possessions we run after. How much of anything does anyone require? Even in people's dreams, their desires follow them, and what is true of individuals is often true in the case of nations. It is not what applies without but within.

I'm a child of God, my success is assured,

my health and happiness is assured.

The spirit of God goes before me

and by peace and prosperity and progress,

I am safe as a child in His love.[1]

The whole universe is in His embrace. The whole galaxy of stars are all within His embrace. He is always for our good, but what is our share? We fail to unify collectively with God. We want Him to act according to our wishes, but we don't want to follow according to His. We want this from God and that from God, then we call Him good. He knows what is better for us and accordingly He dispenses His will.

God is always a dispensation for our good.

In prosperity He tests our virtues,

in mediocrity He tests our contentment and

in adversity He tests our submission.[2]

---

1 and 2   Spontaneously recited verses from memory by Swami Premananda Baba.

Bai Ram

B. HIMACHAL PRADESH

Bai Ram is a follower of the Ramandanda Sampradaya, a strict ascetic sect founded in the thirteenth century by Ramanandacarya. It was only after personally observing her purification and yogic practices that her *sat*-guru,[1] aged one hundred and six, would initiate her into the sect. She explained that at her initiation, her old life ceased and, with it, the concept of age. Bai was at the Kumbha Mela on a bathing pilgrimage and to see other devotees.

"The whole structure of modern society has to change. People just give themselves to society without understanding. They adapt their knowledge and ideas so that they are beneficial to society, but with selfish motives. Where is the service to God? This is the '*Kali-yuga*,' the time of the materialistic and the faithless. If you want to go the way of doubt, God has plenty of time. We believe that you can reincarnate and keep reincarnating up to eighty-five thousand times until you finally learn. Until we return to God, we simply keep on reincarnating. So, if you want happiness and to taste the nectar of life, then you must find the path. For me, that path is complete and total surrender.

You will also need a master to guide you. What really matters in the beginning of your journey is the guru you choose. Be truthful with yourself and have faith in your master. Gather knowledge of the principles of the body and the mind and how they lead to your soul. For your spiritual practice you should be surrounded by the right environment. There is the practice of yoga, which teaches the importance of purifying the mind and body while balancing the *atman*.[2] It is also important to understand some principles of the body and to understand that the food we eat is energy. If you have the wrong principles of the body, the laws of nature will not let you enter higher levels because your energy will run the wrong way. There are three different types of food: *tamasic*, *rajasic*, and *sattvic*. *Tamasic* food is old or fermented food which makes the energy too quiet and low. *Rajasic* food is like meat or hot spices, and this makes the energy nervous. *Sattvic* is pure food, and these foods are vegetables or fruit or simple grains. This is the correct food for spiritual thinking — it will keep your thinking clear and your thoughts clean.

The spiritual road is a very selfless road that you travel, whatever your capacity. The target of my life is truth and beauty and love. Truth is the self, so be honest with yourself in your truth. In truth there is beauty, and the outcome of beauty is love. Love is waiting for you in God. God is kindness, and He shows us His kindness in every moment of existence. Have we forgotten how kind He is?"

1   True or real guru.
2   The true immortal Self and the absolute consciousness of being.

Reverend Kochuparambil J. Kunjumon

B. KERALA

Reverend Kochuparambil J. Kunjumon has been the pastor at the St. John's Church in the Wilderness on British Hill in Forsyth Ganj since 1986. As pastor, he has never once missed giving a Sunday sermon and considers the congregation to be his own family.

"When I was a child, I did not believe in God. I knew that God was our Creator, but I did not like the church. When I was five years old I was taken by a serious illness and my uncle took me to the hospital. The doctor gave his answer: 'No hope.' He said my uncle must take me home to die. At that time my parents made a promise to God that if I did not die, then they would send me for God's work. From five years old until now, my body has never for one day been sick. At the time of the big snowfall here in 1992, four feet of snow fell but I did not use any heater or fire and I was not sick. Then, when I was fourteen years old, I had a dream. In the dream I reached for the sky and heard a sound coming from the middle of the light, telling me what to do. Before that day I did not like reading the Bible, but after that dream I read the book of Genesis through to the book of Revelation. It made a special impression in my heart and I came into a new world.

When I first came here, there was no electricity; only a dog. That is now my dog. I slept here in the church, but the congregation wanted to find a room for me. I said: 'No, I can sleep anywhere and my purpose is not to sleep in a nice bungalow but to preach the word of God.' When I was staying in the church, I heard so many sounds from outside at night. Sometimes sounds like many people coming, sometimes sounds like many horses running, but there are no horses here, and sometimes a sound like a big stone falling on the roof but with no sound falling to the ground. People said the devil was here, and after dark they would not enter the churchyard. For seven days I fasted and prayed. On the last day, at midnight, I took my Bible and walked around the church seven times as He told me, praying like the children of Israel at the Jericho wall. From that day, peacefulness is everywhere and the sounds are gone forever.

I am sitting on this wall talking with you, but my spirit is in the sky with God and the angels and the saints. I am God's child. I receive the light from God and I like to give the light to others. I help the ones who are spiritually blind, flying like kites without any thread. I try to give people the message of the Holy Spirit and to show the way to God. He is like a shining star in the sky when the world is dark. Every day in the morning and evening I take my meditation here in the church. I turn off the lights and I feel like I am in the sky, not alone in the world but receiving Light. When I give sermons, I feel like my whole body becomes bright and the verses are selected and come out of my mouth through the Holy Spirit. I work for the Holy Spirit when I give sermons, so that people can feel the grace of God. My love is for God and He is everything to me. I came into this world alone, and I will return alone, except I have God with me in my heart."

Shree Shree 1008 Kapalik Mahakal Bhairwand Saraswati

B. Punjab

A*kapalika* is a skull, and Shree Shree 1008 Kapalik Mahakal Bhairwand Saraswati has included it in his name because it reminds him that he is a guru who carries the sadness and troubles of all his disciples. As a Vaisnava he has been on his spiritual path for twenty-eight years.

"Faith is to have a spiritual life, and spiritual means God. If God is there, faith is there. In Tantra there are different ways of the same cult. The Vaisnavas, the Gorakhnathis, and the Aghoris are different, because one way is vegetarian and the other not. Meat is eaten by the Aghoris, but only after offering it before the Almighty to be blessed. Vaisnavas never eat meat; we are strictly vegetarian.

You must first understand that true Tantra is not a sexual symbol; it is the supreme worshiping of the Almighty. It is a supreme cult. We wear black as a sign of detachment from the world. It is a color that always remains black, no matter what other colors you put with it. The black robe shows the world that I am firm about my resolution. From the day I joined this cult, I have always worn black — it shows my truth.

Tantra means the chanting of the mantra worshiping the Almighty, and the God deities are Lord Shiva and the Goddess Kali.[1] The mantras are performed ritually and give fruitful results. Tantra is to be chanted and the rituals followed in peaceful places. In temples, cremation grounds, in dense forests, or in the mountains, that is where liberation is to be found by Tantra. Tantra cannot be narrated; it must be seen. The rituals are only performed at night, usually in the cremation grounds for the most peace. One must be a daring person to go into the cremation grounds at night, but we have nothing to fear because our willpower is solid like rock. Everyone has willpower, but in many it is sleeping. Nostradamus was also a Tantric. He was not from the same cult, but he was performing Tantric *sattvas*[2] along the same path. He knew, and we know, that Tantra is the most powerful way to give you mental peace and inner power.

A sense of *samadhi* is like life in a bubble. When you are sitting in *samadhi*, the fact remains that you are not there because you are with God. *Samadhi* links the Brahma chakra[3] to the Almighty, and you become completely detached from the world. Everyone on this earth must seek some self-realization, and self-realization only comes when you think deeply about who you really are and where you come from. By thinking in this way, you will understand that it is possible to detach yourself from the world while living in the world. You live in this world like a lotus flower rising up above the mud."

---

1   Hindu Goddess of Creation and Destruction.
2   Spiritual practices.
3   The highest of the seven chakras, located at the crown of the head.

Baba Balram Das

B. BIHAR

The youngest son of Annapurna Devi, Baba Balram Das[1] lost his left leg from the knee in an indiscriminate shooting incident in a market in Bihar in 1974. He and his mother moved to Vrindavan for his convalescence and they have lived there together since, devoting themselves to their spiritual practices.

"Deep reverence for God is called faith. Without faith, man cannot go toward Krishna. Faith does not come immediately, but through the grace of the guru or the saints. Just like a piece of iron that is put into contact with a strong magnet, the magnetic power enters the iron and a connection is made. So is the case when a man comes into contact with the faithful; the faith naturally enters into his heart.

Truth means Krishna. I have been a devotee since my childhood, when I received the grace of my guru, Sri Sri 108 Baba Sri Radha Govind Das Jee Maharaj. 'Gu' means darkness and 'ru' means repeller, so a 'guru' is one who repels the darkness. The guru makes the connection from you to God. Without a torch, a man cannot repel the darkness of the world. The guru is your guide and he is very necessary. Since I was initiated I have been totally devoted to God my entire life. My whole family — my mother and father and my seven brothers — all surrendered to Krishna. My heart was totally inclined toward Krishna, and since my early childhood I wanted to be a *sadhu*. Not a doctor, not an engineer, but a *sadhu*. A *sadhu* is one who has totally controlled their mind and who does service to Krishna through their mind and body and speech.

When I was a student, I had an accident when I went to the market for purchases. Someone fired a weapon at me without any cause and shot me in the leg. This was by the grace of Krishna, because if he did not snatch my leg, then it was possible that I could be a worldly man of business. It was a very forceful event. I could not finish my Bachelor of Science studies at university because I was a victim of gunfire. My life since my shooting has only been meditation and holy practices.

A material mind has no contact with the true sentiments, for themselves or others; they will even kill beasts for their taste. I do not leave this house to go anywhere except in the service of Radha Govinda.[2] One time I went to Rome, in Italy, because I had disciples there, but I left after fifteen days because I was homesick for Vrindavan. I feel troubled if I leave Vrindavan — not physically, but mentally.

One day a few years ago, I was in a temple here in Vrindavan doing morning service. I washed the floor and bathed the Shiva *linga* of Lord Krishna with milk and curd and honey; this was my duty and my habit. In front of my eyes appeared another Shiva *linga*, right next to the temple *linga*. This was a great miracle for me. Lord Shiva had appeared before my eyes in the shape of the *linga* and I have always kept that small *linga* with me. My happiness is when anyone finds the love of Krishna. When Krishna talks to me, I am always filled with happiness."

1 *"Das"* means servant, and when affixed to a person's name it means "servant of God."
2 Krishna and his consort envisaged as two aspects of the Supreme Deity.

Anila Lobsang Dechen

B. MANALI

Anila Lobsang Dechen has been a Tibetan Buddhist nun since the age of thirteen. She lives in the Gaden Choeling Nunnery in McLeod Ganj near Dharamsala and teaches English to newly arrived nuns who have escaped across the Himalayan border from Tibet. Anila is a first generation Tibetan born in exile.

"Faith is like a light for me, and I go in the direction of that faith, in the direction of the light. I have faith in Buddhism and I practice Buddhism. I have faith in His Holiness[1] and whatever His Holiness says. He is a person who shows me the direction I am going in. Buddhism influences my life and my mind. It tames my mind. All our religious instruction tames and purifies the mind. That is the main practice for a Buddhist nun, to watch your mind. I never question why I am a nun; it does not happen. When I do a job, I keep my motivation clear. When negative emotion arises, I try to tame it. For example, sometimes when I am doing my work, I might suddenly get an emotion like anger or I might say something that I see hurts another person. I say to myself: 'No, that is no good' and I change the direction of my mind. I am just a beginner, but I always try. The philosophy of Buddhism is very deep. Having no spiritual life leads to an imbalance. You need peace in your mind. In materialism, even if you have millions of dollars, you still need a spiritual life — the middle way. There should be balance in your life.

For me, truth means reality. For me, the purpose of being a nun, as in the Buddhist philosophy, is my belief in the next life. So, to benefit from the next life and to prepare for it, we believe in cause and effect, in karma. Spiritual life has tamed my mind so that in the future I will be born a good human, so that I can serve all human beings."

1 His Holiness the Dalai Lama Tenzin Gyatso.

Mahant Narsingh Giri Baba

B. KARNATAKA

Mahant Narsingh Giri Baba was an engineer with a university education before leaving his family in 1972 to become a *sadhu*. He has lived the austere life of an ascetic ever since and wanders from place to place on holy pilgrimages. Giri Babaji is a Naga Baba and was at the Kumbha Mela sharing a tent with other Nagas. They were preparing themselves for the climax of the festival, the ceremonial procession of the *sadhus* for the "emperor's bath" in the River Ganges.

"We are the Naga Babas. Our purpose is to safeguard the *dharma*[1] and our religion. Everyone's aim is separate, but to become a *sadhu* you must leave behind your property and your blood relations. All connections are broken, all temptations are defended — even natural male and female temptations. We have no friends and no enemies; we are all equal. At the time of being born into the Naga life, you are like a living creature experiencing your final death, and then you became clean and reborn like a baby from a mother's womb. If a *sadhu* dies, we do not weep for him, whether it is your brother or your guru. No weeping, only joy. It is a time for celebration when we dig a pit and put him in there.

I have great respect for all living creatures — this is important for every *sadhu*. *Sadhus* are not permitted to see their family or blood relations, because this is a distraction. There would be affection for them because we have the same blood. It is important for us not to remember this connection. We usually do not give our past history or details to anyone, our birthplace or the date, nor our caste, because even that produces powerful emotions. We do not think of our past ever, only of our future. My future is in His hands. Believing heartily, that is the truth — not hearing it or seeing it. If we believe it is the truth, then it is the perfect and final truth. Truth is, of course, God. I have never seen Him, but I do feel Him in nature. Truth and nature are God. Love is blind and I love everything; without love we cannot survive. In *samadhi* you forget everything, including your own existence. You are a body that breathes without breath.

If you really concentrate from your heart, then God will be there anytime — not figuratively; He will be there with you. Without the right connection with Him, you will not feel anything at all. Without belief, you cannot find happiness. Happiness is God's gift and it cannot be purchased anywhere, it can only be earned. My final step is *santi*, peace."

---

1 Sacred duty or righteousness.

Lhakdor-La

B. WESTERN TIBET

As the personal translator and assistant in religious affairs to His Holiness the Dalai Lama Tenzin Gyatso, Lhakdor-La has a pivotal role during the public discourses held annually in McLeod Ganj. It is Lhakdor-La who translates His Holiness's discourses directly from Tibetan into English for simultaneous broadcast on the All India Radio. He is also one of the chosen few who accompanies His Holiness wherever in the world he travels.

"As human beings, as sentient beings, we are all looking for happiness and to remove suffering — to achieve long-lasting happiness. For ages, people have been trying to follow different ways and different techniques; the material way, the spiritual way, and the mental way. Happiness is not necessarily a kind of deluded happiness engaged in all ways of life. The purpose of life is to adopt a way of life and attitude upon which basis you can enjoy happiness and peace, and harm no other person. I think spiritual or religious practice is really very helpful when you are trying to handle the basic source of happiness and the basic source of suffering. Unless we know how to transform the mind, it is almost impossible to achieve long-lasting happiness.

A spiritual life helps to cultivate a proper attitude, and through that attitude you are able to achieve happiness, peace, tranquility, and relaxation. Based on my own limited experience in Buddhism, spiritual practice, or practice to transform the mind, is extremely helpful. It is not easy; it takes many years, and if you are unable to do sincere practice, it would take even longer. To simply be in touch with spiritual teachings, to make an effort to do certain practices, to lead such a life, would bring you tremendous benefit. I think the purpose of my life is to try to bring maximum happiness to the minds of other people and to try to live as happily as I can.

It is by following a spiritual practice that you lead a genuine and sincere life. You do not lead a double life, acting one way and thinking another. This kind of duplicity will disappear, and because you try to live as honestly and as genuinely and sincerely as possible, you will have no record and nothing to hide in life. On the other hand, if you do lead a life of duplicity, you may be able to achieve temporary happiness, but within duplicity you know that you are not right. So, there is no security and no satisfaction. If you genuinely follow the spiritual way of life by being honest and trying to help others as much as possible, you will receive deep inner satisfaction. Truth has many meanings, but I think truth means that there is no gap between appearance and reality."

Avadh Bihari Das Kathiya Baba

B. WEST BENGAL

Seldom venturing far from his camp at the Kumbha Mela, Avadh Bihari Das Kathiya Baba was primarily at the festival to be with some of his eleven disciples. His wooden *langoti* is worn as an austerity and a constant reminder of his faith and vows. The *langoti* is fixed into place so that it cannot be opened until after the completion of the mandatory twelve-year period. His extreme length of real hair, called *jata*, is symbolic of the many years he has engaged in asceticism.

"Love is faith, and in every atom you will find truth. If you have faith and love of God, then your forefathers will guide you in the right way, where everything can be achieved. Here at this Kumbha Mela we have come to do our work, achieving the goals of eternal peace and self-realization. Unless you have realized your true Self, you can never be satisfied, having too many desires that keep itching. Eternal peace is difficult to explain and much, much harder to achieve. One has so many wishes and desires to overcome, so you have to make yourself a companion to this goal. You will have to take every single word and where it originates, where desire originates. You will have to go to that point of origin and there you will have to make an understanding, otherwise you will never get rid of these desires. In meditation, one tries to chant the Holy Name continuously, but trying does not necessarily lead to success. The chanting is going on in the mind, yet the mind is traveling about here and there. Unless you get rid of all worldly desires, you cannot reach closer to eternal peace.

The *langoti* helps us to remember our faith in every moment of every day. The *langoti* is used like one would wear underpants. There are four kinds of *langotis* worn by *sadhus*. *Sutiya* means cloth, a *langoti* made of thread. *Mugliya* is a type of grass, and *sadhus* fold and twist it into thread to make rope and out of that rope they make their *langoti*. *Lohiya* means an iron chain. Those *sadhus* tie a chain around their waist and a flat iron piece for their *langoti*. *Kath* means wood. The Kathiya *langoti* is made so that it is tied around the waist, with a chain around the back which the *sadhu* moves for urination and other things. Without the *langoti* we have no real command over our desires.

At this *mela*, many *sadhus* and saints come from many places to overcome different types of hurdles and to practice meditation. The hurdles that another *sadhu* can easily overcome may take me years to overcome; the opposite is also true. As long as we continue to breathe, we will have to face our hurdles and share our experiences. The sharing of experiences is called *satsang*. We discuss the difficulties in our lives and practices and how God has helped to overcome those difficulties. All my guru's words have been true; this has given me real peace of mind. Peace of mind is something different from everything else. You may have to lie down in the street and make it your home, without family or any attachments, and yet have complete peace of mind. You may be very worldly and

wealthy, yet if you lack peace of mind your life will be unfulfilled and not a real life. This is exactly what makes people like us leave our families and go off seeking peace of mind. Our mental preparation for death as *sadhus* causes us not to bother about it, because we are far removed from such things. It is God's grace. We celebrate death. We get all the *sadhus* together, and we talk and eat at this happy gathering.

The guru has a type of energy that comes along from master to disciple — it is a form of inheritance. My master's master had at least seventy-five disciples and in the end he gave his seat to the youngest disciple — it all depends on who has guru *sakti*. Each and every head of every camp has guru *sakti* — it is a form of energy, a form of God. We call it 'Divine Mother' energy.

Samadhi, in one way, is also like a death. The body will be there, but there is no breathing. Without breath, the body will not change. Every healthy person takes around twenty-one thousand breaths each day, but in *samadhi* the body requires no breath, so it does not change. There are so many paths to God, but the final destination of all the paths is the same and only one.

Truth can only be absolute; there is only one position for truth. Absolute truth can be found here at the Kumbha Mela. One may come seeking it whether one is an aristocrat or a beggar. He will feel it within his own heart if the truth lies there. What it actually is, cannot be explained briefly. I could not explain such an abstract thing even if I were to write a book on the path of truth. It is not possible for me to define truth by adding words together. It does not matter if we are from another religion or from another country or of different appearance, so long as we are walking along the same path. When different religions collide and quarrel, it is because of politics. There is no amalgamation between politics and religion. Truth should be experienced and not defined. Truth will always be truth, without decay or change, whether in the past, present, or future tense. If you expend your time and energy in a proper manner, then it may also happen, even without any initiation into any secular way of worship, that you come to realize the truth. Truth is happening and the truth is to be realized. Water, like truth, only holds the shape of the container it is in. Similarly, truth depends on the container we have made for it in our lives. It takes the shape of the container in which we hold our faith."

Kali Ma

B. SURREY, ENGLAND

Born the black sheep of an English aristocratic family, Kali Ma is a mother, a poet, and the author of published sonnets. She first visited India after being initiated by her guru in 1982. Kali Ma has since spent half of every year on a spiritual pilgrimage in India, which she walks barefoot as part of her austerities.

"Spirituality is to do with your own experience, how you define yourself, and what truth is for you. My truth is that I received 'the knowledge' from my *sat*-guru, who is the last incarnation of Vishnu, and his name is Balyogasha Jagatsat Guru Dev Guru Maharajji. He is a *jagatsat* guru, which means a living guru known worldwide. Maharajji has gone around the world something like thirty-eight times giving people 'the knowledge' and he is only forty. He left India for the West at only fourteen, where he sent out his *mahatmas*.[1]

I first went along to the *satsang*[2] to listen because someone I knew wanted to go and needed a lift. No-one spoke to me at the meeting, so I fell asleep. I went again and noticed that it made me feel good. I felt an energy growing. People were telling me things that nobody had ever spoken to me about before. My interest grew and I began reading the scriptures and it all started coming back to me. Then someone said: 'The Maharajji is coming to England.' I went to see him at the Albert Hall, and received 'the knowledge' on my fortieth birthday. I was so blissed out I couldn't stop smiling. When you get 'the knowledge,' he gives you powerful techniques with metaphysical keys which allow you to feel your true energy. The 'light technique,' for example, goes down your body in waves and makes you feel very clean inside as you feel your past karma leaving you. In the 'music technique,' all of your outward senses are turned inward as your body fills with light. The experience raised my consciousness and I saw a different approach to life. Young people of eighteen are getting 'the knowledge' now and sometimes I wonder why I had to go through all the struggles of life until I was forty before receiving it.

My life in England back then felt like it was going round and round in circles. It wasn't getting me anywhere and it was not the life I wanted. I just sold everything I owned: my house and furniture and cars. My three sons had left home, so I came here to India on a pilgrimage to visit Maharajji's father's ashram. Coming here for the first time was such a cosmic experience.

'The knowledge' is to do with truth; it's a message from the heart. It is to do with love and the unfolding of the universe. I recommend it to everyone — all you have to do is ask for it. The requirements are that you are alive, human, and sincere. It doesn't matter what color or creed or what language you speak. God is love and we all breathe the same air and drink the same water and we all have the same love inside us inherently. We all run on the same energy, including the Maharajji, except he just has a lot more of it. From the first time you go to *satsang* until the time you receive 'the knowledge' is a very beautiful memory. An 'aspirant' is a person who listens regularly to *satsang* and who is aspiring to receive 'the knowledge.' It's like a magnet of love. Maharajji is the perfect master and what you get from him is perfection at the time that it is perfect for you to receive it. I have listened to his *satsangs* over the years and he has never changed his truth. He has never said anything other than that 'the kingdom of heaven is within you.' Maharajji says he is not here to tell people to become vegetarian, or any other trip; he is only here to give people 'the knowledge' if they want it. If anyone can get 'the knowledge,' you are then able to understand so much more of what is going on and know that we are simply going home.

I know now that my whole life was predestined before I was born and, like a seed, I simply unfolded according to my destiny. Time is all an illusion for me. Time is really just one dot, and when you get to that dot it just falls away to where your spiritual consciousness is. I know I am eternal and I trust in the unfolding of the universe by placing myself in the hands of God and my *sat*-guru. The time is short, and where we need help most is in the heart. If we change our hearts, and for many this has already started, we can bring on a 'Golden Age.' God is love, and He comes in many different forms; all we have to do is open our hearts and let His love pour in."

1 Devotees, lit. great souls.
2 Spiritual meeting or gathering of spiritual seekers.

Sri Srimad Bhaktivedanta Narayan Maharaja

B. BIHAR

For more than forty years, Sri Srimad Bhaktivedanta Narayan Maharaja has been a *sannyasin*. He is recognized as a prominent Vaisnava *acarya*[1] and presides over the Kesava Gaudiya Math[2] in the holy city of Mathura. Srila Maharaja has preached extensively in India and has written numerous Vaisnava publications in Hindi. As a spiritual advisor, Srila Maharaja has many thousands of devotees throughout India and in the West.

"There are two types of *sraddha*, faith. One is worldly faith and the other is transcendental faith. Here we only see worldly faith, like being friendly or helping others. With transcendental faith you can enter into devotion with transcendental love. In Krishna you will find a very qualified guru. If I can serve Krishna in any way, my whole life will have been successful, with nothing further to do with anything. Very strongly I have this as my faith.

All worldly truths are false. You are not this body and you think that this body is your soul but, truly, soul is everything and not this body. My name is this and your name is that, but this is not true. Whose house is this? This is my house, but that is quite false. What is your name? Is that the name of your soul? No, this is false. All the truths of this world are false. When you realize your soul, then you can have Krishna as your master. He is my beloved. There is nothing in my life except Krishna — this is true. If I give you money, have I followed my truth? This is false; no-one is the owner of anything, so everything in this world is false. If you have love from your soul to God, then that is true. Transcendental love is not taking, but giving and more giving.

If you are not a realized soul, then you cannot find the true way; everything will be in vain. A person with a realized soul can tell you about devotion, but unless you are developed through spiritual practice, you cannot understand. You will have to practice — it is called *sadhana* — and you will have to chant. As you chant, remember Krishna and bathe in Krishna and by his mercy you will realize truth."

---

1 A person who authoritatively teaches a traditional branch of learning.
2 A Vaisnava monastery.

Sant Sat Guru Dadaji Maharaj

B. UTTAR PRADESH

Sant Sat Guru Dadaji Maharaj is the leader of the Radha Soami faith in Agra. The Radha Soamis are one of many Hindu sects to emerge in India since the beginning of the nineteenth century. As well as a spiritual teacher, Dadaji Maharaj is also an eminent educationalist, having served two full terms as Vice-Chancellor of Agra University.

"Whatever happens in this world is incomprehensible. We perform an action, but we get a different result. With all our modern scientific developments, we cannot account for the way phenomena change our lives. There is something unknown, something omnipresent, something omnipotent and reposing. Faith amounts to a relationship with the unknown, and that unknown can be called the Supreme Being. That inherent relationship which exists between the unknown and the human being is faith. Faith is the basis of all that we do — it is the basis of life. Faith cannot be imposed; faith is something that evolves.

Truth is the Supreme Himself. How do we conceive the spirit? What happens when a man dies? The truth is inherent in the spirit, which leaves the material being and goes off to merge somewhere according to the karmic load it carries. If the load of karma is too heavy, the spirit will have to return to take another human form. On the other hand, with spiritual exercise we are able to realize something within ourselves and, through that realization, we can merge ourselves into the real truth. Spirit is the truth, and anything related to spirit and the Supreme Being is all truth. To merge with the Ultimate Being is to realize the truth of truths. The basis upon which the whole Radha Soami faith rests is the truth of truths. We are here to get ourselves onto the true track, and that quest for truth is the goal of humanity.

Whatever you do materially in this world, whether academically or socially or economically, you may derive some pleasure and satisfaction, but it is always temporary, whereas the satisfaction that you derive spiritually stays with you permanently. To become detached from the material world is the real object of our being. For that there is no need to leave your family life, no need to shun everything and to become a recluse and live in the forest. We are in this world from our eyes to our hands, and from our hearts. We can train ourselves in the technique of detachment. For example, if you hold a pen to paper and begin to write, when you engage in writing, all other thoughts leave your mind as you detach from that which could disturb you. If intellectual attainment is possible through a sort of detachment, then it should also be possible to detach the mind in meditation.

If you are on a spiritual track, doing exercises like yoga or *bhakti*[1] or the attainment of self-knowledge, your spirit is yearning to get closer to the Ultimate Reality. There are so many ways open for the seeker to realize the path that is best for them. Indian mystics have always used reliable forms of meditation to track onto the path of self-realization. To reach any goal, some effort is always

required. If the desire is there, the purpose will become very clear. If a man wants to climb and conquer Everest, he makes the effort, facing insurmountable difficulties, perhaps even risking his life, but still he does it. Similarly, a real seeker of the truth is not bothered by difficulties he faces once he is on the right track. He realizes what cannot be described in so many vivid words and that is called mysticism.

The first step for a seeker, whether from the East or the West, is to pray internally. A desire should be developed so that we realize the Ultimate Reality within this lifetime. For such a realization, there are no barriers of nationality or caste or creed; all are equal. It is the call of the spirit and if that inner call is developed, then there will be no mistakes in life. It is a training, and for that we may need a spiritual teacher. What is a guru? The Supreme Being himself is the real guru. A guru is a person who has realized the Self; who can separate the mind from matter and who can detach and merge with the Supreme. A guru is a person upon whom you can depend. A real guru is never an imposter. He never invites anybody; he lets the seeker come. A person who goes to a spiritual master should have a cautious approach, because there is something important to learn. As experience and knowledge is gained, faith increases and the bond between the student and the master expands.

In the West, people fear death because they follow a policy of escapism by which they want to be removed from death. As death approaches, they are completely shaken because they do not see it as a reality and are therefore unprepared for it. Death is just a natural phenomenon; a person is born, grows, performs actions, and then dies. So, why be scared? Let it come and learn to face it. Rather than fear it, we should prepare for it. Suppose, from our childhood, we know that we have to die and from the beginning of this life our objective becomes to save our spirit? This objective is well within us and we can realize it. Through a technique of detachment, death does not have to be feared.

The Radha Soami faith, which I have been professing for the past forty years, shows you how to face death bravely and how to conquer the fear of death. A human can live for, say, seventy-five years — but what about the spirit? We cannot imagine that; it is unimaginable and therefore beyond conception. The factor known as time does not have a place in spiritual realization. The time factor does not arise; time is just a dimension in which nature behaves. The sense of time limits the self, whereas the spirit knows no limits. Love is also unlimited, and what cannot be limited is not governed by dimensions."

1   Devotion.

Swami Parkash Giri

B. Bihar

Swami Parkash Giri has been a *sadhu* for most of his adult life and, through the practice of *samadhi*, he says he "sits in the lap of God." Swami Parkash spoke to me about meditation as a key to the mystery of life and described *samadhi* as "the special practice of inner wisdom."

"My faith is such that God is omnipresent. He is everywhere and in the hearts of all creatures. Everyone is a form of God. You are a form of God, in this form. I am keenly related to God in every moment of time. I am with my God. Simply feel His loving gaze.

Samadhi means to go into yourself, to break from the outer world and to dive within yourself. There is no mind and no time; you are free. If you take the path to *samadhi*, it is a matter of long practice. First you have to learn through yoga to get rid of all impurities from your body and your mind. You should become too pure. If you are not pure, *samadhi* may cause disease or death. From time to time you will live without food and without drinking. In *pranayama*[1] you will give up breathing also. You will live without air, because there is no need for taking air in that exercise. You must learn to live simply like a stone, and you will learn to drink the nectar of life from nature. Through *samadhi* you will know everything; your mind will be clear. Wherever your mind goes, knowledge will follow. This is the true nature of *samadhi*. Real knowledge will come to you and you will grasp it, just like the clear picture of the cinema.

For the ultimate goal, drinking the nectar of God, there should be no distraction. You should be away from the shadow of women and maintain celibacy. Even touching is prohibited, because women have a current that may inspire sexual attraction and cause a breakage of energy. Society would then be in a position to grasp you. It will make you social and you will not practice yoga. Society will disturb you, and you will turn in your meditation because of ego. For meditation you must clear your mind and go into yourself and your body will become straight. To be totally fulfilled, you will require nothing. Surrender to the lap of God and you will become too cheerful."

---

1 Breathing exercises which regulate the breath.

Yog Mata Keiko Aikawa

B. YAMANASH, JAPAN

Every twelve years, when Jupiter enters Aquarius and the Sun is in Aries, the city of Haridwar on the banks of the River Ganges braces itself for the largest spiritual gathering on earth, the Kumbha Mela. An estimated seven million people converged on the holy city to attend the final Kumbha Mela of this millennium.

One of the most publicized events at the Kumbha Mela was the public exhibition of *samadhi* by a *yogini*[1] from Japan, Yog Mata Keiko Aikawa. Posters on buildings, fences, and trees throughout the city announced the exhibition, to be held at the camp of Maha Yogi Pilot Babaji. Yog Mataji was to be buried underground in a state of *samadhi* for three days without food, water, or air.

From afar the camp of Pilot Babaji had the appearance of a fairground, with huge billowing tents and colored flags flapping in the hot, dry breeze. Inside the gates, one's attention was drawn to a deep pit that had been dug into the hard, pebbly earth for the *samadhi* demonstration. Above the hole, wooden poles supported a thatched roof, which served as protection from the elements. Sturdy railings prevented onlookers from stepping too close, and thick beams placed over the hole formed the structure of a temporary roof. Below, in the dark hole, sat a small, simple table and nothing else.

On the day of the *samadhi*, a throng of excited people gathered to see Yog Mataji, who arrived by car at noon, exactly one hour before her intended burial. She was ushered to a quiet room where she sat in meditation until the appointed hour. A group of dignitaries headed by Pilot Babaji converged, and the procession led Yog Mataji along a grand red carpet to where the enthusiastic crowd had gathered around the pit. The crowd surged forward as Yog Mataji reached the site. Dressed in a light robe, Yog Mataji stood calmly and looked out at the sea of faces before her. They cheered and sang in unison. Standing there, with her hands together in a gesture of prayer, Yog Mataji radiated the serene glow of someone experiencing the euphoric bliss of spiritual ecstasy. As her eyes lost their focus, it became clear that she was already entering the state associated with *samadhi*. When the prayers ended, a ladder was placed in the pit behind her. With an aura of remoteness, Yog Mataji approached the ladder and slowly descended from view. The crowd hushed as the ladder was carefully retrieved. Below, in the pit, Yog Mataji eased herself onto the table in the "lotus position," *padmasana*. Sitting statue-still, her body appeared to have immediately surrendered to a deep meditative state.

Given the signal, helpers placed large sheets of corrugated iron, one overlapping another, onto the supporting beams that formed the roof. When the last sheet was in position, dried palm leaves were layered over the top as men with spades began to shovel earth onto the roof. They continued to shovel the biscuit-colored soil until the mound was almost a meter high. Devotees then gently patted it smooth with their hands. Prayers continued aloud as garlands of yellow and orange flowers were lovingly draped over the mound, forming intricate designs of spiritual symbols. The lively crowd was suddenly still, as though stunned into a collective silence by what they had just witnessed.

In the translucent light of dawn on the following day, the mound stood solemnly in the cold morning mist and the shriveled garlands lay as they had been placed. The sacred site was vigilantly tended by devotees working in relay. Never leaving the site, they maintained its safety and greeted visitors, as news of the *samadhi* display spread through the Kumbha Mela.

By the third day, the atmosphere in Pilot Babaji's camp was filled with tense anticipation, as the curious and the concerned arrived early. The mound remained undisturbed as the sun slowly climbed to its zenith. More people continued to pour into the camp as the moment of truth grew closer. The reassembled dignitaries stood waiting in the shade of a tent until it was time to make their way back along the red carpet to the site of Yog Mataji's *samadhi*. The atmosphere of the crowd was charged with excitement. At precisely 1 p.m. Pilot Babaji gave the signal and men began to dig from the edge of the mound that covered the roof of the pit. It took several minutes of frantic digging before a section of the roof could be cleared and lifted. There, in the darkness below, sitting in the same position that she had been in when the pit was sealed, was Yog Mataji. After a pause she looked up, her eyes half closed against the sharp glare of the sun. She smiled radiantly as helpers eagerly assisted her to view. The crowd erupted in a loud and jubilant cheer.

For the devotees, this was a sacred and faith-affirming event. As she raised her hands in blessing, I noticed that Yog Mataji's robes remained spotless and her composure appeared relaxed. A fragrant garland of red rose petals was placed around her neck as the entourage of dignitaries escorted her through the jubilant crowd. I felt uncomfortable as I thoroughly inspected the hole in the earth in which *samadhi* had just been performed. Nevertheless, I reminded myself of the trickery and deceit I had witnessed during my travels. Intuitively I knew that I would find nothing amiss, but I had to check. The hole itself and the surrounding area remained undisturbed. Not a stone was out of place.

Yog Mataji had publicly performed an extraordinary demonstration of *samadhi* without food, water, or air for seventy-two hours. After resting for just two hours, Yog Mataji was up and receiving guests who had patiently waited to see her. After receiving her blessing, I spoke to Yog Mataji about *samadhi* and the exhibition that had taken place. She said:

"In the universe, everything changes itself. Everything is like a flower: after being beautiful, it drops, becomes the earth, and comes up again. We should use our energy to make beauty; that will help keep us calm. If we poison our lives, we cannot breathe. Poison is everywhere, like jealousy and negative minds. We are always saying that others are no good, but we must see the truth in ourselves. The ego is always fighting and desiring. People only see the surface, but real understanding is when you see the deeper picture. Maybe we die tomorrow. People thinking about money and careers should just once think about their own death. If they died tomorrow, what should they do and how would they prepare? We are all going to die, but how are we going to die? People only think about money. Enough pushing and reacting. It is only when we break that we start to think. Think about God and, through meditation, stop fighting with each other. Ego makes people stupid and pulls them backward. The more spiritual experience you have, the smaller the ego becomes. When you give up the ego, you do not have to resist any longer. People have the largest opinions about the smallest experiences, but there is a bigger experience waiting for them.

In *samadhi* I became myself, free from everything. I became oneness with God. I became light, beyond the mind and beyond the body; everything is dissolved. I became myself, joining the body with the mind. To get to know your Self, that is the highest stage of meditation and yoga. That is self-realization. The mind has many levels, and through yoga we begin to see ourselves change. Having a good-quality body and quality mind, that is what is needed to give service to God. With powerful meditation on peace, we go beyond the physical. One should always send good vibrations. By giving, we become free. The truth is knowing your Self. Material happiness is an illusion. Happiness is without gain; that is how to become detached and free.

It is one long, cosmic road. The soul carries the mind. The mind could be a heavy mind or a light mind — only energy separates them. The soul also has a mind, some kind of energy and consciousness. The reality remains, but our souls return. Pure soul. Surrender is ego-less, where there is no mind to push and react and judge. The more spiritual you become, the more you understand surrender. The world in western life forgets the spiritual, because they are too busy with business and making money. They forget to meditate and other important practices, so they have no guidance along the way. Go beyond the physical — go deeper, and give and take love. Stop and look outside yourself and relax. What we need is more peaceful energy that makes us happy. Return to love and peace. This can all be surrendered to through meditation. Belief is ego-lessness of the self. Truth is love and peace, and we should always hang onto that thought. Give and receive love. Return to love and be in peace."

1   A female yogi.

146

Glossary

acarya A person who authoritatively teaches a traditional branch of learning.

Allah The name of God as recognized by Muslims in the religion of Islam.

asanas Yogic postures that include standing, bending, stretching, and sitting exercises.

ashram *asrama* in Sanskrit. A place of religious study and meditation. A hermitage, monastery, or temple which serves as a shelter for spiritual seekers.

Astanga The name of the eight-limbed yoga as explained by Patanjali in the *Yoga Sutras*.

atman The true immortal Self and the absolute consciousness of being. It also refers to the individual soul.

baba A term of respect for a holy man or spiritual master.

Bhagavad-Gita The "Song of God," a religious poem in eighteen chapters, in which the warrior Arjuna receives Krishna's counsel on *dharma*. It also constitutes the sixth book of the epic Mahabharata.

bhakti Devotion or veneration to the Supreme Lord, a deity, or a guru. It may refer to a spiritual path involving devotion.

bhava-cakra The "wheel of life" or "six realms of rebirth" that constitutes the life forms of existence in Buddhism.

Brahma The Supreme Being in His aspect as the creator of the universe and the first god of the principal trinity in Hinduism.

Brahman The Absolute or Ultimate Reality of Hindu philosophy and God in Hinduism.

Buddha Siddhartha Gautama, born in 563 B.C. in Nepal, found enlightenment under the Bodhi tree and became the Buddha, the "illumined one." He expounded the "four noble truths" as central to his philosophy and his teachings.

chakras *cakras* in Sanskrit. Seven subtle energy centers which transform and distribute subtle energy from the base of the spinal column to the crown of the head.

dandi *dandin* in Sanskrit. A master who has earnt the privilege of carrying a stick or staff.

dharma Sacred duty or righteousness; the eternal order and law of the universe.

diksa Initiation of a seeker into spiritual life by a guru or spiritual teacher.

Ganga The River Ganges. The most sacred river in India to Hindus, it originates in the Himalayas and flows to the Bay of Bengal.

guru Spiritual teacher or master who teaches by example.

ida Passage through which cool *pranic* energy is carried from the left nostril through the body.

imam A leader of Islamic prayer, who is respected as an intermediary between the worshiper and Allah.

japa The repetitive recital of a mantra or holy name as a spiritual devotion, often used during meditation.

jata Length of natural hair matted into "dreadlocks" and worn by ascetics; often indicative of many years of spiritual devotion.

jnana Logical and intellectual knowledge of the world necessary for spiritual wisdom.

karma The universal law of cause and effect. The collective consequences of one's moral and physical actions, in this and other lifetimes.

Koran *Qur'an* in Arabic. The holy book of Islam, divided into 114 chapters of verses. It presents a system of law and theology as revealed to the Prophet Muhammad by Allah in the seventh century.

Krishna *Krsna* in Sanskrit. The Supreme Lord to his devotees. As the most widely celebrated god of Indian mythology, he symbolizes the infinite vastness of universal consciousness.

Kumbha Mela A month-long Hindu festival attended by millions of pilgrims, for a series of sacred bathings. The Kumbha Mela takes place every three years in one of these four holy cities of India: Allahabad, Haridwar, Nasik, and Ujjain.

kundalini Spiritual energy which lies dormant at the base chakra of the spinal column. Once activated, the energy flows up the chakras to the brain, where it manifests as an "awakening" or enlightenment.

langoti Chastity belt worn by ascetics who have undertaken vows of austerity for specific periods of time.

linga Carved phallic symbol used in the worship of Shiva in Hinduism.

Mahabharata The great ancient Indian epic composed between 400 B.C. and A.D. 400. It is divided into eighteen books and includes the Bhagavad-Gita.

mala A string of 108 prayer beads used for the chanting of mantras and holy names.

mantra A sacred word or syllables recited as part of devotional practices. A mantra is said to carry a sound vibration which manifests cosmic energy. The *"Om"* mantra is the sacred syllable most commonly known and widely used in India.

masjid A mosque and place of Islamic worship. Sacred ground where Muslims prostrate themselves in the direction of Mecca five times daily.

maya The deception of appearance and the veil of cosmic illusion.

mufti A position of religious authority in Islam.

Muhammad Born in A.D. 570 in Mecca, he was also known as the Messenger of God and the Prophet of Islam. In his fortieth year, he proclaimed the worship of Allah. His revelations were collected after his death in 632 and later formed the Koran.

Nirvana A liberated state of transcendence indicating another mode of existence. It is the fusion of virtue and wisdom needed to be free from suffering, the goal of spiritual practice in Buddhism.

pingala Passage through which warm *pranic* energy is carried from the right nostril through the body.

prana Breath seen as vital energy that sustains our life force, which is divided into five forms corresponding to their bodily functions.

pranayama Breathing exercises which regulate the inhalation, the retention, and the exhalation of breath.

puja Gathering for ritual ceremonial worship that includes symbolic offerings and the recitation of spiritual text.

rasa The essence of spiritual enjoyment.

rsis A term which refers to seers and saints.

rudraksha The *tulasi* berries used in a string of prayer beads called *japamala*.

sadhaka Spiritual seeker engaged in practices that include yoga and meditation.

sadhana Practices performed by one on a spiritual path that bring about self-realization.

sadhu Ascetic or holy man renounced from worldly life and devoted to spiritual practices, while observing strict rules of conduct that include celibacy.

sadhvi A female *sadhu*.

samadhi A state at the deepest level of meditation in which the mind becomes completely absorbed in the uninterrupted contemplation of reality and ceases to function other than as pure consciousness.

samsara The journey of human existence that repeats itself until the being is liberated from the cycle of rebirth.

samskara Subliminal impressions and consequences from past lives present in this life.

sannyasa *samnyasa* in Sanskrit. The stage of renunciation whereby all worldly attachments and possessions are relinquished in the pursuit of God-realization. Initiation into the renounced order of life.

sannyasin *samnyasin* in Sanskrit. One who has taken the vow of renunciation in pursuit of spiritual liberation.

Sanskrit *Samskrta*, the sacred language of Hinduism in ancient India. Also widely used in Buddhism.

sastra Commentary, instruction, or treatise usually on spiritual text.

satsang Spiritual meeting or gathering of spiritual seekers.

sattvas Practices that embody pure and harmonious spiritual energy.

sattvic Lucidity of mind and purity of body for spiritual practice.

Shaiva A devotee of Shiva; one who carries a trident and a drum, representing destruction and creation.

Shiva *Siva* in Sanskrit. The Supreme Lord to his devotees, he is the god of destruction and the destroyer of ignorance. As the third god of the principal trinity of Hinduism, he is the "king of yogis" who embodies compassion and renunciation.

siddhi Supernatural mystic abilities and the secret knowledge of physical and mental powers.

sraddha The object of devotion and belief, the attitude of faith and conviction.

susumna Channel of subtle energy from the base of the spinal column to the top of the head, through which *kundalini* flows after awakening.

Tantra Rites, texts, and spiritual practices forming one of the fundamental elements of Hinduism. Tantric practices are also found in Buddhism.

tapas *tapasya* in Sanskrit. Penances or severe exercises, which can include austerities and self-mortification.

thanka Tibetan painting on stretched cloth in which the Buddha and *bodhisattvas* are often depicted.

tilak Sacred paint or clay applied to the forehead or body of the followers of Vedic culture.

Upanishads Spiritual treatises of varying length that appear in the Vedas, composed in Sanskrit between 800 and 400 B.C. They formed the principal philosophy of the Vedanta.

Vaisnava A devotee of Vishnu or one of his incarnations who adheres to the scriptures of the Puranas.

Vedanta The philosophy derived from the Upanishads, a scriptural authority of Hinduism.

Vedas A collection of the oldest known scriptures in Indian literature dating to 2000 B.C. They are composed in Sanskrit and are divided into four lengthy parts.

Vishnu *Visnu* in Sanskrit. The Supreme Lord to his devotees, he is the preserver and sustainer of the universe. As the second god of the principal trinity in Hinduism, he is the guardian of the *dharma*.

yoga The union of body and mind through the disciplines performed by *yogis*.

yogi One who practices bodily and mental disciplines. *Yogin* is masculine and *yogini* is feminine.

Bibliography

Brockington, J.L., *The Sacred Thread: A Short History of Hinduism*, Oxford University Press, Delhi, 1992.

Brunton, P., *A Search in Secret India*, B.I. Publications, Bombay, 1980.

Campbell, J., *The Mythic Image*, Princeton University Press, Princeton, N.J., 1974.

Cross, S., *The Elements of Hinduism*, Element Books, Dorset, 1994.

Fischer-Schreiber, Ingrid; Ehrhard, Franz-Karl; Friedrichs, Kurt; Diever, Michael S., *The Encyclopedia of Eastern Philosophy and Religion*, Shambhala Publications, Boston, 1994.

Flood, G., *An Introduction to Hinduism*, Cambridge University Press, Cambridge, 1996.

Glassé, C., *The Concise Encyclopedia of Islam*, Harper & Row Publishers, San Francisco, CA, 1989.

Hartsuiker, D., *Sadhus, Holy Men of India*, Thames and Hudson, London, 1997.

Harvey, P., *An Introduction to Buddhism: Teachings, History and Practices*, Cambridge University Press, Cambridge, 1990.

Maitreya, B.A., *The Dhammapada*, Parallax Press, Berkeley, CA, 1995.

Miller, B.S., *The Bhagavad-Gita: Krishna's Counsel in Time of War*, Columbia University Press, New York, 1986.

Nyanaponika, Thera, *The Heart of Buddhist Meditation*, Rider & Co., London, 1969.

Osborne, A., *Ramana Maharshi and the Path of Self Knowledge*, B.I. Publications, Bombay, 1979.

Rahula, W., *What the Buddha Taught*, Grove Press, New York, 1959.

Raju, P.T., *The Philosophical Traditions of India*, Motilal Banarsidass Publishers, Delhi, 1992.

Shearer, A., *The Hindu Vision: Forms of the Formless*, Thames and Hudson, London, 1993.

Spielberg, F., *Spiritual Practices of India*, Citadel Press, New York, 1962.

Taimni, I.K., *The Science of Yoga*, Theosophical Publishing House, Madras, 1965.

Zaehner, R.C., *The Bhagavad-Gita: With Commentary Based on the Original Sources*, Oxford University Press, London, 1969.

Acknowledgments

This book, from conception to completion, has been a constant source of inspiration for me. What began as a photographic quest, unfolded and resulted in a spiritual journey that became an act of devotion, the experience of which will always remain in my heart. My gratitude to the beautiful people of India whose paths I crossed on my sojourn, for their kindness, friendship, and their willingness to be of assistance.

My deep gratitude to the men and women who are the subjects of the photographic portraits, for their trust and generosity in sharing knowledge and wisdom from their sacred lives.

———

I would especially like to thank my wife Karyna, for her extraordinary love, her integrity of spirit, and her sustained loyalty. I thank her for giving me the inspiration for this book and for editing the selection of photographs.

———

I sincerely wish to thank the following people in Australia for their significant contribution toward the manifestation of this book:

Nevill Drury at Craftsman House, for his vision and encouragement of my proposal from the beginning.

Anna Voigt at Craftsman House, for her assistance with the text and personal insights.

Hari Ho at Fine Arts Press, for his technical and production advice.

Caroline de Fries at Fine Arts Press and Kirsten Smith, for their creativity in designing the book.

Claire Armstrong at Fine Arts Press and Robyn Flemming, for their careful editing and proofreading.

Dr. Peter Oldmeadow, Lecturer in Sanskrit and Classical Indian/Buddhist Thought at the University of Sydney, for his invaluable assistance with the text and the Sanskrit terminology.

Julie Stokes at the National Library of Australia in Canberra, for her assistance with the text.

Roger W. Scott for his exquisite interpretation of the film and expertise in producing the black-and-white prints.

Cathy Cresswell and Lyndsey Hope at Business Backup Centre, for their infinite patience and attention to detail in the typing of the drafts.

———

This book was also made possible through the kind sponsorship of:

Kodak Australasia. Thanks to Peter Rattray.

Nikon/Maxwell Optical Industries. Thanks to John Swainston and Jann Hott.

———

I would also like to thank my mother, Josephine, for her unconditional love and support throughout my life.